THE FORMATION OF
THE NEW TESTAMENT

Religion

Editor

THE REV. PROFESSOR E. O. JAMES

M.A., D.Litt., Ph.D., F.S.A., Hon.D.D.

*Formerly Professor of the History and Philosophy
of Religion in the University of London*

The Formation of the New Testament

ROBERT M. GRANT

*Professor of New Testament and Early Christianity
at the Divinity School of the University of Chicago*

HUTCHINSON UNIVERSITY LIBRARY

LONDON

HUTCHINSON & CO. (*Publishers*) LTD
178–202 Great Portland Street, London, W1

London Melbourne Sydney
Auckland Bombay Toronto
Johannesburg New York

★

First published 1965

*This book has been set in Times New Roman,
printed in Great Britain on Antique Wove paper
by The Anchor Press, Ltd., and bound by Wm.
Brendon & Son Ltd., both of Tiptree, Essex.*

Contents

Preface

The New Testament is the basic collection of the books of the Christian Church. Its contents, unlike those of the Old Testament, were produced within the span of a single century, under the auspices of disciples of Jesus or their immediate successors. The collection is also unlike the Koran in that it contains not a word written by the founder of the community, though his spoken words are recorded by evangelists and apostles and reflected in almost all the documents. The New Testament is thus the product of tradition, and it contains the records of the life, teaching, death, and resurrection of Jesus and the earliest, classical responses to this many-faceted event. The various books were created within the Christian community and gradually came to be accepted by almost all the individual churches which constituted the Church.

When we speak of the formation of the New Testament we refer to the gradual process in the course of which the various books came to be collected and circulated and finally to be recognized as making up the authoritative record of the apostolic witness to Christ. In essence, this process was the work of Christians in the second century. Debates over the authority of some of the documents sporadically arose in later periods, but the main outlines of the New Testament became clear to most Christians by about the year 200.

Not all Christians used the same terminology or definitions, but in general the authoritative New Testament books were those which (1) were, and had been, accepted by orthodox churches and church writers, (2) were regarded as written by apostles or disciples of apostles and, (3) could, like the Old Testament books, be called inspired 'scripture'. There is a definite correlation between the development of the idea of canonicity and emphasis on the Church as Catholic and apostolic.

The New Testament was thus created by the Church in the sense that Christians chose the books which, in their view, adequately represented the life and thought of the primitive community. Obviously this view was not shared by those who produced most of the apocryphal gospels, epistles, acts, and apocalypses which more orthodox Christian leaders rejected, and often we tend to suppose that the less orthodox were occupying themselves with creative fiction. This was certainly not what they intended to produce. They generally believed that they had inherited a tradition which was not available to all, and there are passages in the synoptic gospels (especially in Mark 4:11, 33–34) which suggest that there was such a tradition. Some of them, like Marcion, believed that the earliest apostles had distorted the original tradition in order to make it relevant to their earliest hearers. As Christian leaders defined and defended the New Testament books they insisted that the authentic tradition contained in them was comprehensible to all and available for all. Even though they sometimes had to engage in highly subtle exegetical manœuvres in support of this contention, they insisted that the gospel was universal in scope and they were often suspicious not only of Gnostic documents but also of the more esoteric New Testament writings such as Revelation (in the East) and Hebrews (in the West). The very difficulty of these books may account for the persistent doubts about their canonical character.

The New Testament is not the product, however, of official assemblies or even of the studies of a few theologians. It reflects and expresses the ideal self-understanding of a whole religious movement which, in spite of temporal, geographical, and even ideological differences, could finally be united in accepting these twenty-seven diverse documents as expressing the meaning of God's revelation—in Jesus Christ and to his Church.

One may wonder why the formation of the New Testament needs to be examined again. This question can be raised on two counts. (1) The early history of The New Testament canon was exhaustively investigated during the late nineteenth century and the early twentieth. Why do it again? (2) The New Testament canons of various churches are already in existence, and it is most unlikely that they will ever be altered.

The first question is easier to answer than the second, and the answer is twofold. (a) We now possess some new materials, chiefly from Egypt (second-century Christian papyri; later Gnostic books which have earlier sources), which provide new light on the formation of the New Testament. (b) The continuing study of early Christian life and literature has tended to discredit older theories of straight-line development and also to lay more emphasis on the close relation between Gnosticism and more orthodox Christianity in the second century. This means that the history of the canon must be viewed from a new perspective.

The second question is related to modern theological concerns which, in turn, have been influenced by historical considerations. (a) Tradition as such is not valued in the modern world as highly as it was in previous times. The fact of a past decision remains; its significance often becomes relative because of our search for the factors which motivated it and our desire to look behind the decision and reassess its causes and its importance. (b) Continuing study of tradition suggests that it would be better to speak of 'traditions', usually congruent but by no means identical. Throughout church history some New Testament books have been valued more highly than others, under varying circumstances. By reviewing the process of canonization we become able, using historical imagination, to see how and why various books were regarded as authoritative—and thus to free ourselves from the notion that all scriptures are equal. (c) This is not to say that our valuation will necessarily be the same as that of any early Christian writer. It is simply to point to the freedom with which, in many instances, the books (or the traditions underlying them) were used and by analogy to suggest that modern readers possess a similar freedom.

It is significant that as these books came to be generally accepted, there was also a crystallization of the Church's organization and of its doctrines. To speak of the creation or formation of the Catholic Church in the second century would be an exaggeration. The ingredients of the Catholic Church were present from the beginning, even though no New Testament writer used the term or, for that matter, viewed doctrine or organization in just the same way as did the second-century theologians and administrators. But while we should insist upon the elements of continuity within the Christian tradition and traditions, it would be quite wrong to suggest that the faith of Irenaeus, for example, was identical with that of the New Testament writers as a group or that of any particular one of them. The different circumstances required the use of different accents and emphases.

While we can view the New Testament books as containing the classical responses of the apostolic age (and the sub-apostolic age) to Christ, the same approach can be made to the Church for and in which these books were written, and in the early history of the Church's canon we can see both continuity and adaptation. The first century or century and a half of the Church's life are not marked by fixity, by preciseness in definition, or even by universal agreement about organization.

To examine the early history of the New Testament canon means to investigate the early history of the life of the Church—and to see that flexibility, conflict, and (to a remarkable extent) diversity was the consequence (or perhaps a cause) of being alive.

The gradual development of the canon, in our view, was primarily the achievement of gentile Christianity, although of course there would have been no New Testament if an Old Testament had not already existed. Among the earliest Christians there was no New Testament; their Bible consisted of the Old Testament alone. One of the principal problems which the Church had to confront during the second century was the relation between this Bible and the Christian gospel expressed in oral traditions and in writings. Gentile Christians insisted upon the superiority of the gospel to the predictions and prefigurations which they found in the Old Testament, and this insistence finally led to the formation of the New Testament as a collection of books which could be viewed as 'scripture'.

Our study could obviously not be undertaken apart from the advances made during the last century of biblical and patristic research. For the late nineteenth century and the early twentieth the names of Harnack and Zahn remain crucially important. Among modern scholars we may mention especially J. Ruwet on Clement and Origen, W. C. van Unnik on Gnostic writings (and non-Gnostic writings as well), and H. Koester on the Apostolic Fathers.

I

The scriptures of the earliest Church

Our study of the formation of the New Testament in the early Church is concerned with the books which early Christians read. They began with the Old Testament, as the rather literary-minded Luke indicates in his picture of Jesus in the synagogue at Nazareth. Jesus 'was given the book of the prophet Isaiah, and opening the book he found the place where it was written, "The Spirit of the Lord is upon me . . ." ' (Luke 4:17–18; Isaiah 61:1). Similarly in Acts 7:42 we hear of the 'book of the prophets', a reference to the Jewish book of 'the Twelve Prophets', including Amos, from which a quotation follows. In Acts 13:33 we find a precise reference to 'the second Psalm'—a reference which in some manuscripts has been corrected to 'the first Psalm' because the two psalms were sometimes run together (as in Justin, *Apol.* 40, 8–18). This evidence is enough to show that Luke, at least, was greatly concerned with Old Testament prophecy and referred to particular passages with some care. Similarly the evangelist Matthew depicts important events in the life of Jesus as taking place so that particular prophecies, carefully quoted, might be fulfilled. There is no reason for us to labor this point, or to inquire whether early Christians used the prophetic writings as wholes or in the form of selections of 'testimonies'—or in both ways—since it is enough to state that for the early Church 'scripture' primarily meant the Old Testament.

Naturally enough, the Old Testament books were quoted in order to lay emphases on predictions or prefigurations of the life of Jesus and of the Christian community. This is to say that Christians found prophecy throughout the Old Testament, in a fashion not unlike that of the Qumran community, where prophecies were viewed as largely fulfilled in the work of the Teacher of Righteousness. Such interpretations, indeed, are to be found in much of the Jewish apocalyptic literature of this period. The Old Testament pointed forward beyond itself and either had begun to be fulfilled or was just about to be fulfilled.

Since the New Testament books which reflect the life of early Christians are written exclusively in Greek, it is not surprising that most of the Old Testament quotations in them are derived from the Greek Old Testament, the Septuagint; but sometimes, for example in the Gospel of Matthew, some of the quotations seem to be based on different renderings of the Hebrew text. Recent archaeological discoveries have shown that the Septuagint was in circulation even in Palestine, and that its text was somewhat different from that found in the major, later manuscripts. Undoubtedly the Palestinian Greek manuscripts underwent a good deal of correction on the ground of comparison with Hebrew texts, and it may be that New Testament passages which seem to be closer to the Hebrew than to the Septuagint are based on corrected Septuagint texts.

The Old Testament books which the earliest Christians read, however, were those which are contained in the Hebrew Bible. Clear references or allusion to other books, as we shall see later, are found only in Hebrews, James and Jude. In general the earlier Christians restricted their reading to 'the law of Moses and the prophets and the Psalms'

(Luke 24:44), although with the Psalms was included the book of Proverbs (cf. Rom. 12:20).

It is quite possible that the earliest Christians wrote letters and memoranda or other documents,[1] but the oldest one to survive—if it is authentic, as it appears to be—is a letter from the Church of Jerusalem to gentile Christians in the vicinity of Antioch (Acts 15:23–29), about the year 47.

> The apostles and the elders, brethren, to the gentile brethren in the vicinity of Antioch and Syria and Cilicia, greetings.
>
> Since we have heard that some persons coming from us have disturbed you with words, unsettled your minds (although we gave them no instructions), it has seemed good to us in assembly to choose men and send them to you with our beloved Barnabas and Paul, men who have given up their lives for the name of our Lord Jesus Christ. We have therefore sent Judas and Silas, who themselves will tell you the same things by word of mouth.
>
> For it has seemed good to the Holy Spirit and to us to lay upon you no burden except these necessary matters: for you to abstain from what has been sacrificed to idols, from blood, from what is strangled, and from fornication. If you keep yourselves from these, you will do well. Farewell.

This four-part letter follows the general pattern of Greek official decrees. It begins with a salutation, describes the circumstances under which the decree has been voted ('it has seemed good to us in assembly'), gives the decree itself ('it has seemed good . . . to us'), and ends with a brief 'farewell'.

Authentic Christian literature as we know it, however, begins with the letters of the apostle Paul, perhaps about the year 50. These letters are often regarded as 'occasional'

1 Compare the letters Paul received from the high priest (Acts 9:1–2, 14).

in the sense that he wrote them in haste and for specific situations. Such a classification is partly true, partly inadequate. It is true that specific occasions called forth the responses expressed in the letters; but the letters do more than set forth the encounters between Paul's mind and the situations. They come out of a fairly long period of life and thought in the Christian community, and in them Paul invariably passes beyond the specific situations to expound the implications of Christian faith for himself and for his readers. They are 'tracts for the times', to be sure, but they express insights not specifically limited to the local churches or to the middle of the first century; this is why copies of them were kept.

Before writing the major letters now preserved—Romans, 1–2 Corinthians, Galatians—Paul had been a zealous defender of Jewish orthodoxy for some time; he had been a Christian convert for nearly two decades, and had worked as a missionary, often among gentiles, for at least fourteen years. The letters, therefore, do not contain the spontaneous effusions of a neophyte. They reflect the considered opinions of a highly intelligent, deeply Christian leader with heavy responsibilities for the welfare of the communities under his direction. His critics were well aware of this fact. 'His letters,' they said, 'are weighty and powerful, though his physical presence is ineffective and his speech is contemptible' (2 Cor. 10:10). The letters do not suggest that they were written in haste. Instead, they contain carefully reasoned arguments and admonitions, and in many instances they reflect considerable pains in matters of style and structure. Paul was no Greek rhetorician but he could and did write in such a way as to communicate his understanding of the gospel to his readers.

We may admit that the outline of his letters is not always transparent. No doubt he did not always follow an outline.

In some cases, however, the situation is different. The thanksgiving at the beginning of 1 Corinthians suggests that he knew in advance most of the themes he was going to discuss. So does the statement about 'the gospel', along with the thanksgiving, in Romans. The introductions to 2 Corinthians and Galatians are somewhat less closely related to the later parts of the letters, but in Galatians it would have been inadvisable to give away the whole line of argument at the beginning.

How did Paul actually write his letters? In spite of a vast amount of work on this subject, the answer is still not altogether clear. What we actually know can be stated rather briefly.[1] While 1–2 Thessalonians certainly express the thought and even the style of Paul, they were written in the names of Paul, Silvanus, and Timothy, and in 1 Thessalonians Paul only occasionally differentiates his own statements from those of the others (2:18, 3:5). At the end of 2 Thessalonians (3:17) he himself adds that 'the salutation is in my handwriting: "of Paul"—this is an indication in every letter; thus I write'. This remark clearly points to the inference that in 1 Thessalonians 5:27 the words 'I adjure you by the Lord to have this letter read to all the brethren' are Paul's, and that probably the whole conclusion of 1 Thessalonians was written by his hand. It seems likely that the bulk of these letters were dictated rather than actually written by the apostle.

In 1 Corinthians, again, the salutation is written in Paul's own hand (16:21), and this fact suggests that when he uses the word 'I write' (5:11) he has dictation in mind. Perhaps such is also the case in 2 Corinthians 13:10 ('I write'). The

1 In order to set forth the evidence, certain assumptions have to be made. The assumption made here is that Paul was the author of ten epistles, written in the following sequence: 1–2 Thessalonians, 1–2 Corinthians, Galatians, Romans, Philippians, Colossians (with Philemon), Ephesians.

situation in Galatians is a little more obscure. Paul says to his readers, 'See with what large letters I write [or, I have written] with my own hand' (6:11). Since the subject changes at this point, and since Paul moves on to a conclusion of the whole letter, it is often supposed that he began writing here after dictating what went before. This supposition is probably correct, especially in the light of what has been said about salutations; but it remains possible that he actually wrote the whole letter.

Romans presents a special problem. Romans 15:15—'on some points I have written to you very boldly'—proves nothing one way or another. Romans 16:22, however, provides some remarkable information. It is not from Paul at all but has been added by a scribe. 'I Tertius greet you, I who wrote the letter in the Lord.' Now it has often been thought that Romans 16 does not belong with the rest of Romans but constitutes a separate letter; on this basis Tertius would not necessarily have anything to do with Romans 1–15. This theory seems wrong. It is inconceivable that a Pauline epistle could have consisted of practically nothing but greetings, as Romans 16 does. Instead, it clearly provides the conclusion for the letter as a whole; it indicates who was to carry the letter (Phoebe of Cenchreae, 16:1–2), and Tertius inserts his greetings not because he has just written something comparable to a postcard but because he has been Paul's scribe over an extended period of time.

The imprisonment epistles contain no indications about the work of scribes, but Colossians ends with a salutation in Paul's own hand (4:18), and in Philemon 19 Paul writes a personal IOU which is apparently different from the writing in the rest of the letter. We may assume, then, that these letters were dictated.

We conclude that Paul's usual practise was to dictate the the bulk of his letters to a scribe and often to add notes in his own handwriting, perhaps also correcting what the scribe had written.

It may be worth noting that arguments from analogy on this subject are not very convincing. Ancient writers resembled modern writers in this regard: sometimes they wrote for themselves, sometimes they dictated. The Roman orator Cicero preferred to do his own letter-writing, but sometimes he used scribes. In Acts 15:23 the apostles and elders of Jerusalem are described as 'writing through the hand' of Judas and Silas, and these men are obviously messengers (15:27). Peter is described as writing 'to you through Silvanus' (1 Pet. 5:12), and while it is not impossible that Silvanus carried the letter, it is more likely that he was the scribe. When Polycarp tells the Philippians that he has written them 'through Crescens' and then commends Crescens to them (Phil. 14:1) it is clear that Crescens is to be a messenger. It is not so clear, however, how Ignatius wrote his letters. He wrote to the Romans 'through the blessed Ephesians' and named one of them as 'very dear to him' (Rom. 10:1); perhaps this man was to carry the letter. He wrote to the Philadelphians (11:2) and the Smyrnaeans (12:1) 'through Burrhus'; this probably means, as Walter Bauer argued,[1] that Burrhus was to carry the letters to the communities involved.

The use of the word 'through' in this regard is rather ambiguous. If we take the case of 1 Clement, a letter of the Roman church to the Corinthian church, we find its author describing his own words as 'said by God through us' (59:1) or as 'written by us through the Holy Spirit' (63:2). The ultimate author is God; the intermediate author is the composer of the letter. Nothing is said about a scribe. Similarly, when Dionysius of Corinth speaks of the same letter as

1 *Die Briefe des Ignatius von Antiochien und der Polykarpbrief* (Tübingen, 1920), 254.

written by the Roman church 'through Clement'[1] he has authorship, not penmanship, in mind.

Only in the third century does the composition of Christian literature come to involve the *systematic* use of copyists, and such use seems to have begun when Origen's wealthy admirer Ambrose, eager to have him produce commentaries on scripture, 'supplied him with more than seven shorthand writers who relieved one another at fixed times, and as many copyists, as well as girls skilled in penmanship'.[2] When Origen wrote a theological letter to Africanus, Ambrose himself took part in the dictation of the letter—not, one would suppose, by actually writing it down himself— and then corrected it for his friend.[3] Finally, after Origen had gone to Caesarea and was more than sixty years old, he permitted shorthand writers to take down his public discourses.[4] In recent years the final copy of such a discourse has turned up on papyrus—the *Discussion of the Father, the Son, and the Soul with Heracleides and the other Bishops*.

We have discussed this rather late evidence not to suggest that it is analogous to what we find in the Pauline epistles, but instead to indicate the variety present in various situations. It may be urged, however, that inasmuch as Paul did use copyists it is not unlikely that he retained copies of his own letters, or that his lieutenants did so, thus making the task of collecting his letters easier.[5]

Once his letters were written, they were not entrusted to the postal service. The Romans had no postal service except for the transmission of government mail. Instead, local messengers would often take a letter to the congregation being addressed (1 Cor. 16:17–18; Phil. 2:25–30). Sometimes

1 Eusebius, *H. E.* 4, 23, 11.
2 *Ibid.*, 6, 23, 2.
3 *Ep. ad Africanum* (Lommatzsch XVII, 48).
4 Eusebius, *H. E.* 6, 36, 1.
5 Perhaps 2 Timothy 4:13 has something to do with this.

one of Paul's lieutenants would carry such a document (2 Cor. 8:16–24; Eph. 6:21; Col. 4:7–9). The deaconess Phoebe probably carried Romans (Rom. 16:1); the runaway slave Onesimus carried the letter to his master Philemon.

Paul was sometimes concerned with the reception and public reading of his letters. To the Thessalonians he swears 'by the Lord that the letter should be read to all the brethren' (1 Thess. 5:27), and in Colossians 4:16 he gives instructions for this letter to be read not only at Colossae but also in the church of the Laodiceans, while the Colossians are to read the letter they receive from Laodicea. It may be that Paul warns the Thessalonians against forged letters circulating in his name (2 Thess. 2:2; cf. 3:17).

Naturally the correspondence went both ways, though none of the letters to Paul from the churches has survived (a letter from the Corinthians to him is a second-century forgery). Clear proof that Christians wrote to him is provided in 1 Corinthians 7:1, where he speaks of matters about which they had written. In addition, some members of the community provided him with unwritten information (1 Cor. 1:11). What we find in his letters is only a part of a much larger exchange of ideas, as countless passages show, to mention only 1 Thessalonians 3:4, 4:6; 2 Thessalonians 2:5, 3:10; and Galatians 1:9.

Paul's letters, of course, were not the only specifically Christian documents which the early Church possessed, even though they are the only ones we know from the fifties of the first century. Somewhat later we encounter other letters, such as the one addressed by (or in the name of) Peter to the 'Dispersion sojourners' of Pontus, Galatia, Cappadocia, Asia, and Bithynia (1 Pet. 1:1), the general epistle written in Peter's name and containing a reference to itself as a 'second letter' (2 Pet. 3:1), and three letters apparently written by John, with frequent use of the verb 'to write'.

These examples indicate that Christians were becoming increasingly self-conscious about literary processes, and we are therefore not surprised to find an injunction about reading in Mark 13:14 and emphasis on Jesus' reading in Luke 4: 16–20. Indeed, Luke's gospel begins with a statement about the author's sources and purpose (1:1–4) which recalls similar passages in the writings of Hellenistic historians (see also Acts 1:1). Towards the end of the Gospel of John there is another statement of purpose: 'Jesus performed many other signs . . . which are not recorded in this book; but these are recorded so that you may believe . . .' (John 20: 30–31). And in John 21:24–25 someone (an editor?) has testified to the reliability of the book's sources and has explained that the world itself could not contain all the books necessary for recording all of Jesus' actions. This last comment is intended to tell why other books contain other materials.

In addition, the Book of Revelation is described as a written work of prophecy (1:3); it begins with seven stylized letters to churches (1:11), later on contains repeated injunctions to 'write' (14:13, 19:9, 21:5), and ends with a solemn curse laid upon anyone who adds to the content of the book or subtracts from it (22:18–19).

We get a few further glimpses of early Christian literary creativity when we look at some of the writings of the so-called Apostolic Fathers, most of whom flourished in the early second century or, in the case of Clement of Rome, at the end of the first. The letter we know as 1 Clement was specifically directed by 'the church of God sojourning at Rome' to 'the church of God sojourning at Corinth' and was carried to Corinth by three Roman Christians, named at the end of the work. More copies were soon put in circulation, however, since Ignatius, a few decades later, probably knew the letter and his contemporary Polycarp of

Smyrna knew it practically by heart (perhaps it was preserved at Smyrna, from which Ignatius wrote several of his own letters). It was also treasured at Corinth, as the later bishop Dionysius tells us, and towards the end of the second century it was certainly known by Irenaeus of Lyons, who had visited Rome, and by Clement of Alexandria.

Ignatius of Antioch wrote letters to four churches (three in Asia Minor, one the church of Rome) from Smyrna, on his way to a Roman martyrdom; from Troas in Asia Minor he wrote three more. He had intended to write letters to all the churches on the route ahead of him (Rom. 4:1), but when he found he could not complete his task because he was abruptly sailing from Troas to Neapolis he asked Polycarp of Smyrna to write on his behalf (Polyc. 8:1). From a later letter of Polycarp to the Philippians (13:1–2) we know that Polycarp did write to this church and that the Philippians replied to him, sending a letter through him to the church of Antioch and asking him for a collection of Ignatius' letters. The seven Ignatian letters which we now possess were obviously collected by Polycarp and sent to Philippi; this is why most of the manuscripts of Ignatius' letters also contain Polycarp's covering letter. The letters of the bishop of Antioch were given an *imprimatur*—though quite an unofficial one—by the bishop of Smyrna.

A similar semi-official approval was given to part of the *Shepherd* of Hermas, at least the part which Hermas say she copied from a little book which an old woman—the Church —gave him in a vision (Vis. 2, 1, 4). Before he had given his copy 'to the elect of God', the old woman appeared to him again and told him that she had more to say. 'When I have finished all the words they shall be made known through you to all the elect' (2, 4, 2). The way in which this 'publication' was to take place was made very explicit: Hermas was to write one little book for Clement to send to 'the cities outside'—this reminds us of the transmission of 1 Clement to the Corinthians and perhaps to other churches —and one for Grapte, who would instruct the widows and orphans at Rome from it. Hermas himself was to read the book at Rome 'with the presbyters who govern the church' (2, 4, 3).

In Hermas' description we find portrayed the activities of a Christian layman who saw visions and reported them to the authorities of the Roman community. Presumably they gave their stamp of approval, for otherwise it would be hard to imagine how Hermas' work would have been—as it was —rapidly transmitted to various Christian communities, including (by the end of the second century) those at Lyons (Irenaeus), Antioch (Theophilus), and Alexandria (Clement).

These three kinds of documents (church/church: 1 Clement; bishop/church: Ignatius and Polycarp; and layman/church: Hermas) doubtless do not exhaust the kinds of writings there were, but they show us that there was at least this much diversity. The situation in the first century was probably not dissimilar; all we know about it suggests that it was much the same.

It is most unlikely that any of the New Testament books were written later than the beginning of the second century, and most were probably completed before the year 80. Unfortunately, our information about the life and thought of the Church during the last quarter of the first century is very limited, and if we try to describe the way or ways in which the New Testament books were being used and transmitted during this period we must rely in large measure on inferences, hypotheses, and guesses. In later chapters (IV–VI) we shall turn to what is known about the very last years of the first century and the early years of the second. Here, however, we shall try to set forth what we can imagine to have been happening in the period before the Apostolic Fathers wrote.

G. Zuntz has made the interesting point that in 1 Clement (about 95) there is a paraphrase of Romans 1:29–32 (1 Clem. 35:5–6) which ends with the words 'Those who do [*prassontes*] these things are hateful to God—not only those who do [*prassontes*] them, but also those who share in approving them.'[1] The text is clearly based on Romans 1:32—the word *prassō* occurs there but not elsewhere in 1 Clement—though not on Romans in the original form but close to what is read in the Beatty papyri (*P* 46). Here we have our oldest reflection of Romans 1:32, from a Christian community which had received the letter only forty years earlier from Paul himself; but the text has been corrupted. Perhaps the change is due to an early copyist; perhaps it derives from Paul's own scribe.

Such possibilities lead us to wonder how the Pauline epistles may have been collected. Apart from the Pastorals and Romans, all those we possess are addressed to communities in a relatively restricted area—on the western shores of the Aegean Sea (Corinth, Philippi, Thessalonica) and in western Asia Minor (Laodicea [?], Colossae, Galatia). It is conceivable that the letters were collected by Christians in the focal center of Asia Minor, Ephesus, and—in any event—probable that such a collection had been made by the time when 2 Peter was written; for in it (3:16) we read of 'all the epistles' of Paul, and the context suggests an allusion to 1 Timothy 1:16. This point indicates that toward the end of the first century a collection of Pauline letters was in existence, though we do not know that such a collection was universally accepted or that there were not various collections in existence.

It has sometimes been suggested that when such a collection

1 *The Text of the Epistles* (Oxford, 1953), 219–20.

was made it may have been headed by I Corinthians, and that at that point some 'universalizing' words were added to Paul's salutation. He would have addressed only the Corinthian Christians, while an editor would have added 'with all those who call upon the name of our Lord Jesus Christ in every place, their [Lord] and ours'. Hans Lietzmann, however, drew attention to Jewish synagogue inscriptions which contain the words 'peace be upon this place and upon every place of [the people] Israel'. Paul himself, not an editor, is therefore making use of a Jewish formula of blessing; the blessing is universal, but his letter is intended for the Corinthians.[1] There is thus no evidence to support this theory about the collection.

Another theory, much more ingenious, was produced by E. J. Goodspeed about thirty years ago.[2] In his view there were no collections of the Pauline letters until a concern for Paul's writings arose, about A.D. 85, because of the publication of the Acts of the Apostles. At that point a devoted Paulinist from the Lycus valley in Asia Minor—a man who already possessed Colossians and Philemon—procured a number of the letters, either by correspondence or by actual visits, from communities with which, according to Acts, Paul had been closely related. As a kind of 'introduction to Pauline theology' the same person produced Ephesians, based largely on Colossians and other letters, to go at the beginning of his collection. Goodspeed's theory has one important foundation stone in the New Testament. Colossae is not mentioned in Acts; the other communities addressed in the Pauline epistles are mentioned there. It is easier to move from Colossians to the collection, so to speak, than to explain why Colossians would otherwise be included in it. To this conjectural explanation Goodspeed added—with

1 *Texte und Untersuchungen* 68 (Berlin, 1958), 284–87.
2 *The Meaning of Ephesians* (Chicago, 1933).

the assistance of John Knox[1]—the further hypothesis that the collector was Onesimus, since this is the name of the runaway slave in the letter to Philemon and, as well, of the bishop of Ephesus in Ignatius' time (a half century later).

There are several difficulties with this theory. (1) Could Acts have stimulated interest in Paul's letters? It never mentions any of them or describes Paul as writing to churches. (2) Ephesians may well be an encyclical letter—or was it, as Marcion conjectured, written to the Laodiceans? It is by no means certain, in any event, that Paul did not write it himself. (3) It is difficult to believe that communications among the Christian communities of the first century were so limited that they did not exchange apostolic letters, especially since Paul himself refers in 1 Corinthians 16:1 to what he had told the churches of Galatia and elsewhere gives news about one church to another (e.g., 2 Cor. 8:1) and instructs the Colossians to exchange letters with the Laodiceans (Col. 4:15–16).

On balance, we are inclined to reject this hypothesis, even though we must then admit that we have nothing equally ingenious to substitute for it. In later chapters we shall consider the evidence which actually exists in the writings of the Apostolic Fathers. For the moment, however, we wish to disregard it and offer imaginative possibilities as to the way or ways in which the New Testament writings were handed down in the latter half of the first century. We have already suggested that one, or perhaps more than one, collection of Pauline letters was in existence and in circulation (2 Peter). The situation as regards the gospels is not so clear. If we were to assume that the tradition is correct which relates the Gospel of Mark to Rome, then we might well proceed to argue that when this book came to be known

1 *Philemon Among the Letters of Paul* (Chicago, 1935)

elsewhere—and such would probably have been the case very early, because of the centrality of the capital city—it would then (1) have been read in conjunction with other traditions about Jesus, oral and/or written, and next (2) have been combined with these traditions in written form. In this way it would be possible to explain the origin of the Gospel of Matthew, perhaps in Syria, and the Gospel of Luke, according to late tradition in Greece. The fact that Mark was not used in the Gospel of John would suggest that John lived and wrote in a community where Mark was not known, perhaps in Palestine, or else that John and/or his readers were so firmly convinced of the authenticity of his gospel that they were not concerned with relating Mark to it.[1]

It should also be noted that the 'period of oral tradition' did not come to an end when written gospels were produced. Luke certainly knew written narratives about the life of Jesus (1:1), but he did not feel that they contained all the traditions that existed; in Acts 20:36 he quoted a saying of Jesus which he did not report in his own Gospel. Similarly, John (20:30) refers to 'signs' performed by Jesus but not recorded in his work. And it is well known that not only among Gnostics but also among more orthodox Christians 'unwritten' sayings of Jesus continued to circulate in the late second century and afterwards.

We must therefore envisage a situation in the latter half of the first century in which Mark circulated rather widely but in a context in which were found not only other written gospels but also continuing oral traditions. In some localities local traditions were combined with Mark; in other localities they were not. The evidence for combining Mark with other traditions is to be found in the gospels of Matthew and Luke and, in addition, in the two additional versions of

1 Except perhaps, by implication, in John 20:30–31 and 21:25.

Mark to which the fragment of Clement of Alexandria discovered by Morton Smith refers: one, a distinctively Gnostic, precisely Carpocratian version; the other, a version used in secret by the church of Alexandria. The fact that Smith's fragment speaks of these versions of Mark, and that we never learn elsewhere of various versions of Matthew[1] or Luke or John, seems to point toward the widespread and early dissemination of this Gospel alone.

It is therefore all the more surprising that, as we shall see in Chapter III, there are practically no traces of Mark among the Apostolic Fathers, except in the writings of Papias of Hierapolis. We must therefore make a further assumption—that after Mark was sent forth it was almost immediately combined with local traditions of various kinds and that the newer gospels, more complete and more meaningful than Mark, soon came into circulation and replaced Mark's work. In Rome itself, collections of oral traditions (in writing or not) were employed; at Antioch, there were the gospels of Matthew and John, and perhaps Luke, as well as oral traditions. Finally, we suggest that in all these localities, as well as in others, there was probably present a mixture of books and oral traditions, and that the fact that we can trace (with some measure of confidence) the presence of particular books in the particular writings we possess does not prove that other books were not in use. Our evidence is too severely limited for us to be able to erect lofty edifices of inference upon it.

As for the circulation of the non-Pauline epistles and the Revelation of John, we know practically nothing. We may suppose, however, that Hebrews, which is somehow related to Italy (13:24), would be read at Rome—and Clement of Rome did read it. 1 Peter, sent in the apostle's name to

---

1 The idea that the Gospel of the Hebrews was the original of Matthew is a rather late, learned conjecture.

various churches in Asia Minor (1:1), would have been preserved among them and at Rome as well, and no doubt was
circulated from Rome to other churches. By the time the
author of 2 Peter wrote, he could produce a very general
epistle and can refer back to 1 Peter as universally known
(3:1). Since he made use of Jude, another general letter, in
his own epistle, we may assume that he wrote from a locality
in which such documents were collected (cf. also a possible
allusion to John 21:18 in 2 Peter 1:14) and from which they
were sent—perhaps Rome. The three Johannine epistles may
represent the contribution of Asia Minor, and the Revelation
of John, with its introductory letters to seven Asia Minor
churches, certainly comes from that area. The epistle of
James is harder to place, but it is highly probable that it
represents (in its present form) a document, or group of
documents, preserved at Jerusalem. The fact that tangible
proof of its existence is not available before the end of the
second century may reflect only the gaps in our information;
it may also point to a certain lack of contact between
Jerusalem and other churches.

There are two passages within the New Testament books
themselves which may suggest that their authors regard
other apostolic or sub-apostolic documents as 'scripture' in
the sense in which the Old Testament was scripture. Both
passages are found in letters which are ascribed to apostles
but seem to have been produced at a somewhat later time.
The first is 1 Timothy 5:18, a verse rather similar to 1 Corinthians 9:9. Both epistles deal with Deuteronomy 25:4,
'You shall not muzzle an ox threshing grain,' and refer it
to payments to Christian ministers, but in 1 Timothy we
read that 'the scripture says, "You shall not muzzle . . .",
and "the workman deserves his wage" '. Obviously the
author regards the second quotation as derived from scripture—and it is found in Luke 10:7. It is possible that by

'scripture' he means Deuteronomy 25:4 and that he regards the second quotation as exegesis of it. Alternatively, he is really quoting from Luke as scripture; in this case, his letter must have been written after the composition of Luke, which (since the book is partly based on Mark) brings us to a date in the last quarter of the first century. It could well be that he is using the word 'scripture' in a rather free way —as in 2 Timothy 3:15-16, where Timothy is described as having known 'sacred writings' from infancy and these sacred writings are composed of 'every inspired scripture'.

The other passage, in 2 Peter, is also fairly imprecise. The author, writing a general letter with no particular readers in mind, speaks of regarding 'our Lord's long-suffering as salvation, as our beloved brother Paul . . . wrote to you' (3:15). The passage he has in mind seems to be 1 Timothy 1:15-16, and if this is so, for him the Pauline epistles include the Pastorals and are regarded as addressed to all Christians, not just the original recipients of the letters. Furthermore, the author of 2 Peter speaks of 'all his [Paul's] epistles', and describes 'the ignorant and unstable' as mis-interpreting not only these letters but also 'the other scriptures' (3:16). For the author, then, there is a collection of all the Pauline letters, and it can be regarded as 'scripture'. Unfortunately there is no obvious clue to the date or the situation in which 2 Peter was written. The earliest clear trace of its use by any Christian writer occurs in the works of Origen (third century), and while we should certainly not suppose that it first came into existence at that time, there is no reason for regarding it as prior to the last decade of the first century or, for that matter, the opening decades of the second. Another situation in which the Pauline epistles were used in this way is to be found in the letter of Polycarp (see Chapter VI).

II

The Old Testament canon
in Judaism and Christianity

For the earliest Christians 'scripture' consisted of the Old Testament, and one might suppose that in order to create their own canon of scripture all they had to do was to take the Old Testament canon as recognized by Jewish leaders and add to it a collection of specifically Christian books. The process was not so simple, however, for among non-Christian Jews there were varieties of usage and there seems to have been no attempt to settle the question as to a precisely defined canon until well after the fall of Jerusalem in A.D. 70.

Judaism

This not to say that there was not a collection of books generally accepted. When the Dead Sea sectarians collected passages in which they found predictions of the future related to their own destiny, they confined their attention to such Old Testament documents as Genesis, Exodus, Numbers, Deuteronomy, Joshua, 2 Samuel, the Psalms, Isaiah, and Amos.[1] Evidently they were relying on authorities

1 For these collections see J. M. Allegro in *Journal of Biblical Literature* 75 (1956), 174–87; 77 (1958), 350–54.

recognized not only by themselves but also by other Jews who might ask them questions. There was something like an Old Testament, prior to the sect and to its competitors.

Our earliest evidence for the existence of an Old Testament is to be found in the prologue to the Greek translation of the Wisdom of Sirach (Ecclesiasticus), written about 130 B.C. The translator speaks of 'the law and the prophets and the other ancestral books'. From Sirach itself (cc. 42–50) it is plain that there was a collection which included the five books of Moses and the historical writings, Isaiah, Jeremiah, Ezekiel and the twelve minor prophets, Psalms, Proverbs, and Chronicles—perhaps Job as well. In 1 Maccabees 12:9 (about 100 B.C.) we hear of 'the holy books', though we are not told what they are.

The existence of this collection, however, was not equivalent to the existence of a fixed canon of Old Testament books in the sense that nothing could be added to it or taken away from it. This fact is made especially clear by the discoveries of the Dead Sea Scrolls, for at Qumran there was a range of sacred literature much wider than what we have encountered in Sirach. The composition of sacred books, often regarded as secret, was continued, especially by writers of apocalypses who wanted to ascribe their own views to authors who lived long before them. The Apocalypse of Enoch (1 Enoch) provides the most notable example.

Generally speaking, the New Testament writers confined their reading to the books most widely accepted by contemporary Jews. This is the situation we find mentioned in Luke 24:44: 'the law of Moses, the prophets, and the psalms'. On the other hand, some New Testament writers clearly went beyond these limits. In Hebrews 1:3 there is a clear reflection of the Wisdom of Solomon (7:25–26), while in Jude 9 there is a paraphrase of the apocryphal Assumption of Moses and, in Jude 14–15, a quotation from 1 Enoch 1:9.

B

An unknown writing is cited as scripture in James 4:5. This is to say that there was a collection of books generally received, but no canon absolutely fixed.

A tripartite division like Luke's is to be found in the treatise *On the Contemplative Life* written by the first-century Alexandrian Jew Philo. We hear of 'laws and oracles, delivered by prophets, and hymns and the other [books] by which knowledge and piety are mutually increased and perfected'. Most of Philo's quotations from the Old Testament are taken from the Pentateuch; but in his writings there are no references to Ezekiel, Daniel, Ecclesiastes, the Song of Songs, Esther, Ruth, or Lamentations—not to mention the books later regarded as apocryphal. In this respect it is probably significant that Ezekiel, Ecclesiastes, the Song, and Esther encountered criticism made by various rabbis at a later date, and that in the New Testament there are no allusions to the last three books. In other words, both Philo and the New Testament writers seem to reflect collections of Old Testament books which in some measure were more restricted than was the case among other writers of the first century.

The first definite picture of an Old Testament canon which we possess is that provided by the apologist Josephus in his treatise *Against Apion*, written at Rome between A.D. 94 and 96. This is what he says (1, 38–40):

Among us there are not countless discordant and conflicting books, but only twenty-two, containing the account of all history and rightly given credence. Five of these books are by Moses; they contain the laws and the tradition from the creation of mankind up to his death (a period of about 3,000 years). From the death of Moses to [the time of] Artaxerxes king of the Persians, the prophets after Moses composed the history of their times in thirteen books. The remaining four contain hymns to God and moral precepts for men.

Josephus' mention of Artaxerxes shows that he has in mind the book of Esther, in which this king plays a prominent part. We do not know exactly what the other books were which he included in his groups of thirteen and four: but the most natural assumption, in view of lists later ascribed to Jewish sources, is that the thirteen were made up of Joshua, Judges–Ruth, Samuel, Kings, Chronicles, Ezra–Nehemiah, Esther, Job, Daniel, Isaiah, Jeremiah–Lamentations, Ezekiel, and the Twelve, while the hymns and precepts were found in Psalms, the Song, Proverbs, and Ecclesiastes.[1]

It is sometimes supposed that Josephus reflects an 'Alexandrian' canon of the Old Testament because, as in the Septuagint version—the most popular Greek version of the Old Testament in his time—Ruth follows Judges and Lamentations follows Jeremiah. The same situation is to be found, however, among Jewish informants of Origen (Eusebius, *H. E.* 6, 25), and we do not know that they were following Alexandrian tradition. The fact that later rabbis placed Ruth and Lamentations in a special division called Kethubim, or 'writings', does not show that earlier rabbis did so. Indeed, the number of books Josephus insists upon suggests that he is following Hebrew sources, for there are twenty-two letters in the Hebrew alphabet.

But while Josephus' collection may well have been as 'canonical' as he insists it was, the number of the books in the Jewish canon was not definitely fixed. Arguments about Ezekiel, Proverbs, Ecclesiastes, the Song, and Esther seem to have continued after Josephus' time; and in the apocalyptic 2 Esdras (4 Ezra), composed in the last decade of the first century, we hear of a collection of ninety-four books, seventy of which are secret, while twenty-four are openly

---

1 H. E. Ryle, *The Canon of the Old Testament* (London, 1892), 165–66; T. Reinach-L. Blum, *Flavius Josèphe Contre Apion* (Paris, 1930), 10 n. 3.

published (14:45–48). This number is also found in the Babylonian Talmud (*Baba Bathra* 14b), in accordance with a tradition which probably goes back to the second century of our era. The difference between twenty-four and twenty-two is due to the separation of Ruth from Judges and of Lamentations from Jeremiah.

In our opinion, however, the content of the Hebrew canon was well enough settled after the time of Josephus and 2 Esdras; the minor variations are not especially important. Presumably the agreement between these authors is due to the crystallization of opinion in late first-century Palestine, especially under the influence of the sages who taught and discussed such matters at Jamnia. A council held there about A.D. 85–90 considered the nature of the canon, though the nature of its conclusions is not absolutely clear.

Christianity

Christians were often much concerned about the nature of the Jewish canon of the Old Testament, especially as they came to be aware that after Jamnia it was more clearly defined than it had been earlier. Some Christians were concerned because of their close ties with Judaism; others, because in debates with Jews they had to use authorities accepted by their opponents.

A document reflecting the ideas of the former group and apparently originating in the second century has been reconstructed by J.-P. Audet.[1] He relied on lists found in a Jerusalem manuscript of the year 1056 (this manuscript, first published in 1883, contains the *Didache*) and in Epiphanius' treatise *On Weights and Measures*. In this list there are

1 'A Hebrew-Aramaic List of Books of the Old Testament in Greek Transcription', *Journal of Theological Studies* I (1950), 133–54.

twenty-seven Old Testament books, with titles given in Greek and in Hebrew or Aramaic.

1. Bresith (Genesis)	15. Debri iamim
2. Elesimoth (Exodus)	(Chronicles [I])
3. O[d]oikra (Leviticus)	16. Debri iamim
4. Of Jesus (Joshua)	(Chronicles [II])
5. Eledebarim	17. Of Proverbs
(Deuteronomy)	18. Of Koheleth (Ecclesiastes)
6. Ouidabir (Numbers)	19. Sir asirim (Song of Songs)
7. Of Ruth	20. Of Jeremiah
8. Of Job	21. Of the Twelve
9. Of Saphtin (Judges)	22. Of Isaiah
10. Spher telim (Psalter)	23. Of Ezekiel
11. Of Samuel, I	24. Of Daniel
12. Of Samuel, II	25. Of Esdras, I
13. Of Kings, I	26. Of Esdras, II
14. Of Kings, II	27. Of Esther

The names of the books of the Pentateuch (into which Joshua, with a Greek title, is mysteriously inserted)[1] are given in Hebrew, as are the Psalms, Chronicles, and the Song of Songs. Some of the other names are definitely Aramaic (Judges, Kings, and Proverbs), and this, along with the fact that 'of' represents the Aramaic genitive particle, suggested to Audet that the list was based partly on Hebrew texts and partly on Aramaic translations or 'targums'. In any event, the list obviously originated among Jews or Christians who spoke Hebrew and Aramaic and then was used among Christians who also spoke Greek.

From our standpoint the sequence of titles has some rather peculiar traits; but we must remember that in the second century the arrangement was still fairly fluid. Melito of Sardis will show us the sequence Numbers/Leviticus. In Audet's opinion the arrangement of items 7–16 (Ruth–2

1 More simply, Numbers and Joshua are simply transposed.

Chronicles) is 'haphazard',[1] but it may reflect an attempt to put Job in the time of the Judges; such a notion is ascribed to Rabbi Eleazar in *Baba Bathra*.[2] Similarly, the Psalms may be placed before the books of Samuel because of their supposed Davidic authorship; another Jewish list provided by Epiphanius (*Pan.* 8, 6, 2) gives the sequence Judges–Ruth–Job–Psalms, then the three books ascribed to Solomon. These three books, in Audet's list, more naturally follow Chronicles. The order of the prophetic books is rather strange, presumably because it was not definitely fixed; and Esther may come at the end because of doubts as to its canonical status.

In any event, these are the Old Testament books probably accepted by Jews and by Jewish Christians alike in the second century. It can be supplemented by a list which Eusebius copied from the *Selections* of Melito, bishop of Sardis in Asia Minor about 170.[3] Melito tells us that there were questions as to the true number and the true order of the Old Testament books, and that he had undertaken a pilgrimage to Palestine in order to acquire correct information, apparently from Greek-speaking Jewish Christians. His list is as follows:

Of Moses, five books: Genesis, Exodus, Numbers, Leviticus, Deuteronomy;
Jesus Nave (Joshua), Judges, Ruth;
of Kingdoms, four books;
of Chronicles, two books.
Of Psalms of David [one book?].
Proverbs of Solomon, also called Wisdom; Ecclesiastes; Song of Songs; Job.
Of prophets: of Isaiah, of Jeremiah, of the Twelve in one volume; Daniel, Ezekiel, Esdras.

1 *Ibid.*, 150.
2 Ryle, *op. cit.*, 277–78.
3 *H. E.* 4, 26, 13–14.

As in Audet's list, the titles are a little peculiar, but there is no interrelation between the two. Melito's use of the word 'of' has nothing to do with Aramaic, for he is using Greek titles, as his classifying of Samuel and Kings together as 'Kingdoms' shows. He also takes pains to indicate that when his readers hear of a book of Wisdom they should think not of the apocryphal Wisdom of Solomon but of the book of Proverbs. (In this regard Jewish Christian usage was to differ from that of other Christians.)

According to P. Katz, the question of the exact number of the books with which Melito was concerned is really irrelevant. Jewish usage was not fixed at this time, and a good deal of the variety we encounter is due to different ways of counting various volumes.[1] There is also a good deal of error in various lists because of the carelessness of copyists. This fact may explain Melito's omission of the book of Esther, although there may have been doubts about it among Christians as there were among Jews.[2]

The question of the order of the books was also, really, impossible to settle. If there were variations even within the Pentateuch, how could one expect the works ascribed to David and Solomon, or the writings of the prophets, to retain a fixed sequence? Perhaps the remarkable thing is that Proverbs, Ecclesiastes, and the Song of Songs stayed together, as did Isaiah, Jeremiah, and the Twelve (in varying orders) and Daniel–Ezekiel (sometimes transposed).[3]

To some extent the evidence we have found in Audet's list and in Melito can be supplemented by what Justin, arguing

1 *Zeitschrift für die neutestamentliche Wissenschaft* 47 (1956), 191–217.

2 Clement of Alexandria (*Str.* 1, 123, 2) speaks of Esther and Mordecai 'whose book is in circulation as is that of the Maccabees'. This probably points to doubts about Esther's canonical status.

3 Another list, derived from Jewish sources by Origen (Eusebius *H. E.* 6, 25, 1–2), adds little but further confusion.

with a Jewish opponent, provides about 160 in his *Dialogue with Trypho*, since he explicitly claims that he is arguing on the basis of books accepted by Jews. It is thus fairly significant that he explicitly mentions the books of Genesis, Exodus, Leviticus, and Kingdoms (with a quotation from 1 Kings); he also speaks of the Psalms and refers to five of them by their numbers in the Greek version. Like Melito, he refers to the Proverbs of Solomon as 'Wisdom' (*Dial.* 129, 3); he also quotes from, and names, the book of Job. Among the prophets he refers to Isaiah, Jeremiah, Ezekiel, and Daniel, as well as to the Twelve Prophets. In addition, his remarks about the text of Esdras show that Jews accepted at least one book by him (*Dial.* 72, 1). Books out of which Justin takes quotations or allusions, without naming them, include Numbers, Deuteronomy, and 2 Chronicles.

We lack references or allusions to Judges–Ruth, Ecclesiastes, the Song of Songs, and Esther. The absence of Judges–Ruth must be due simply to Justin's mode of argument, since there is no reason to suppose that the authority of these books was ever questioned. On the other hand, questions were raised about the last three books in Jewish circles, and this fact may account for his silence in regard to them. His evidence is highly tantalizing, for it is plain enough that he could have answered our questions about these 'marginal' books had he wished to do so. It is clear, however, that all the Jews he knew used the major Old Testament books.

It should also be said that outside Alexandria a collection of Old Testament books essentially Jewish in origin and nature was employed, although with occasional additions. Theophilus of Antioch gives us quotations from twelve Old Testament books and alludes to others in such a way as to provide testimony to everything except Leviticus, Numbers, Judges–Ruth, Ecclesiastes, the Song of Songs, and Esther. Once more, there seems to be no reason for his having to avoid the first three, but since he was strongly influenced by Jewish ideas he may have preferred not to use the last three. In addition, he definitely alluded to the book of Baruch (sometimes also read by Jews) and perhaps to Tobit.

Similarly his contemporary Irenaeus reflects knowledge of all the Hebrew Old Testament (in Greek) except for Ruth (often combined with Judges), the books of Chronicles, Ecclesiastes, the Song of Songs, and Esther. Though it may seem unlikely that he could have rejected the books of Chronicles, they do not appear in the earliest Christian Syriac version of the Old Testament, and they may have been absent from some Greek Bibles. As we have already seen, there were difficulties about the last three books mentioned, and they do not really come into their own in Christian circles until the beginning of the third century.

We may suspect that these later Christians avoided Ecclesiastes, the Song of Songs, and Esther both because these books are not employed in the New Testament and also because their teaching had little to offer Christians except when, in regard to the Song of Songs, allegorization was strongly employed. This is to say that for Christians as for Jews the idea of 'scripture', at least in regard to these books, was less important than the question of religious and theological content.

Apocrypha and Pseudepigrapha

In addition to the books generally accepted by Jews, there were also sectarian documents, chiefly apocalyptic in nature, which were enthusiastically accepted in places like Qumran. Among these were such books as 1 Enoch, Jubilees, the Aramaic Testament of Levi, the Psalms of Joshua, and anthologies of Old Testament texts. Some of these works were used by Christian writers either before or after the closing of the Jewish canon. Furthermore, there were books which were not quite canonical but were used sometimes by Jews, sometimes by Christians, and sometimes by both groups. Origen, for example, tells us that 'outside these'— the canonical books—'are the Maccabaean books, which are entitled *Sarbeth Sabanaiel*'. The meaning of this Hebrew title is not absolutely certain, but it is evident that Origen has a Hebrew text of 1 Maccabees in mind. This book had been used by Josephus for historical information; it re-appears in the writings of Tertullian, Hippolytus, and Origen. Again, 2 Maccabees was used by Philo of Alexandria, and it is reflected in such Christian writings as Hebrews (11:35) and works by Clement, Hippolytus, and Origen. Traces of 3 Maccabees are harder to find. It is copied in the fifth-century Codex Alexandrinus, but when three books of Maccabees are mentioned in the fourth-century *Apostolic Constitutions* (8, 47, 85) the books in view may be 1, 2, and 4 Maccabees. The semi-philosophical 4 Maccabees is found both in Codex Alexandrinus and in the fourth-century Codex Sinaiticus; Eusebius (*H. E.* 3, 10, 6) mentions it, and very probably it was known to Ignatius of Antioch, early in the second century.[1]

There were also various books ascribed to Baruch, sup-posedly the contemporary of the prophet Jeremiah. According to the *Apostolic Constitutions* (5, 20, 3) 1 Baruch, found in the Septuagint manuscripts Vaticanus (fourth century) and Alexandrinus, was read by Jews when they commemor-ated the destruction of the temple; but there seems to be no trace of it in Jewish literature. On the other hand, it was certainly used by Christians—most of whom ascribed it to Jeremiah—for there are allusions and/or quotations in the works of Athenagoras, Theophilus, Irenaeus, Clement,

1 See O. Perler in *Rivista di archeologia cristiana* 25 (1949), 47–72.

Hippolytus, and Origen. The early second-century apocalypse known as 2 Baruch had a singular history among Christians; Papias of Hierapolis ascribed some of its teaching to Jesus (Irenaeus, *Adv. haer.* 5, 33, 3–4), while a quotation from it in the Epistle of Barnabas is assigned to a prophet (11:9). A fourth- or fifth-century papyrus fragment in Greek (P. Oxy. III 403) may have belonged to a Christian at Oxyrhynchus. Finally, another apocalypse known as 3 Baruch *may* have been known to Origen (*De princ.* 2, 3, 6).

1 Baruch is a wisdom-book, and there were several other such books about which Jews, if not Christians, were rather uncertain. The Wisdom of Sirach (Ecclesiasticus) is quoted as scripture in the Talmud, though not all Jews accepted it; it seems to lie behind some passages in the *Didache* and 1 Clement, and both Clement and Origen frequently made use of it. It is found in the Septuagint manuscripts Vaticanus, Sinaiticus, and Alexandrinus. The Wisdom of Solomon, on the other hand, does not appear in ancient Jewish writings. It was used by such Christians as the author of Hebrews (1:3), Clement of Rome, Ignatius, Athenagoras, Irenaeus (only once, however), Tertullian, Clement, and Origen. Indeed, the Muratorian list (probably late second century) seems to treat it as part of the New Testament!

Two other books not unlike wisdom literature were not used by Jews in Origen's time, according to his letter to Africanus. These are Tobit and Judith. Tobit, however, was clearly employed by the author of 2 Clement and by Polycarp, perhaps by Theophilus, and certainly by Clement, Hippolytus, and Origen. The Ophite Gnostics (Irenaeus, *Adv. haer,* 1, 30, 11) regarded Tobias, the hero of the book, as inspired by the angel Eloi (Elohim); presumably they were reacting either to Jewish or to Christian use of the book. Similarly Judith was known to Clement of Rome, Clement of Alexandria, Tertullian, and Origen.

We should also mention the apocalypse known as 2 Esdras or 4 Ezra, used in Barnabas (12:1) and in the *Shepherd* of Hermas, as well as by Clement of Alexandria (*Str.* 3, 100, 4). This work was taken over by Christians at some point after its composition late in the first century, for the first two chapters and the last two, lacking in oriental versions, are clearly Christian in nature.

Finally, in the Septuagint version there are additions to various Hebrew books. These additions, not accepted among the Jews, were clearly used by Christian writers who presumably were relying only on a Greek translation. Among them we may mention (1) the Song of the Three Holy Children, added to Daniel, which is reflected in 1 Clement and definitely accepted by Clement of Alexandria and Origen; (2) the story of Susanna used by Clement of Alexandria and defended by Origen against the criticisms of Julius Africanus; (3) the tale of Bel and the Dragon, accepted by Irenaeus, Tertullian, and Origen; (4) additions to Esther, first attested by Josephus and later accepted by Clement of Rome, Clement of Alexandria, and Origen; and (5) the Prayer of Manasses, found in the Syriac *Didascalia* (third century) and the *Apostolic Constitutions* (2, 22, 12–14), as well as in the Codex Alexandrinus.[1]

For our purposes it is not so important that most of the writings we have mentioned are reflected at Alexandria by Clement and Origen, at the end of the second century and the beginning of the third, as that some of them are echoed in the writings of the Apostolic Fathers, at the beginning of the second century and, in some cases, at the end of the first, and in New Testament books. We have already mentioned the fact that Hebrews definitely contains an allusion

1 For later use see H. Volz in *Zeitschrift für Kirchengeschichte* 70 (1959), 293–307.

to the Wisdom of Solomon, possibly also to 2 Maccabees, and that in Jude there is some use of apocalyptic literature. One of the best witnesses to early Christian use of a fairly extensive Old Testament collection is Clement of Rome, who wrote to the Corinthians toward the end of the first century.

Clement's primary Old Testament authorities are the Psalms, Job, Isaiah, Genesis, and Proverbs, though he also quotes from Exodus, Deuteronomy, Jeremiah, Ezekiel, Daniel, and Malachi, paraphrases passages from Numbers, Joshua, Esther, and Judith, and alludes to the Wisdom of Solomon. Four quotations come from unidentified, by definition apocryphal, sources. Clement never names the books he is using, and sometimes he mixes up his quotations in a way that suggests he is relying either on rather vague memories or on an anthology without reproducing its references. If he is using such an anthology, it contained some apocryphal sayings but not, it would appear, materials from Esther or Judith or the Wisdom of Solomon; these are his own contribution. The basic 'canon' which underlies Clement's letter is the Jewish canon, although apocryphal materials have been introduced into it (8:3, 17:6, 23:3–4, 46:2). One apocryphal work to which 1 Clement refers as 'scripture' (23:3) is cited as 'the prophetic word' in 2 Clement 11:2; it therefore belonged to Clement's Old Testament.

A rather different situation is to be seen in the Epistle of Barnabas. Here we find clear and definite quotations from all five books of the Pentateuch, from Psalms and Proverbs, and from the prophets Isaiah, Jeremiah, Ezekiel, Daniel, and Zechariah, as well as from 1 Enoch, 2 Esdras, and 2 Baruch. There is probably an allusion to the Wisdom of Solomon (20:5), but no quotation from it. Barnabas mentions Enoch and paraphrases several verses from his book (4:3), also quoting from it as scripture (16:5), and he speaks of the authors of 2 Esdras (12:1) and 2 Baruch (11:9) as prophets. His canon, it would appear, consists of the books generally accepted by Jews—plus at least three Jewish apocalypses.

We do not gain much information about the Old Testament from Ignatius or Polycarp, although Ignatius provides two quotations from Proverbs as scripture (Eph. 5:3; Magn. 12). An allusion to Isaiah 52:5 (Trall. 8:2) shows us how freely the Old Testament was often quoted. In the Septuagint the text reads thus: (1) Because of you (2) constantly (3) my Name (4) is blasphemed (5) among the gentiles. Phrases 2–5 are repeated exactly in 2 Clement 13:2a, and 1, 3–5 with slight modifications in Romans 2:24. In 2 Clement 13:2b, apparently, the same verse is quoted again in another form: Woe (to him) because of whom my Name is blasphemed; and variants of this occur in Ignatius and in Polycarp (Phil. 10:3). It is possible that the 'woe' form actually comes from some apocryphal document; but it is so similar to the verse in Isaiah that it seems more likely to be the same thing in another form.

We cannot deny, of course, that the Apostolic Fathers did make use of apocryphal documents. Indeed, the only explicit quotation in the *Shepherd* of Hermas comes from the lost *Book of Eldad and Modat* (Vis. 2, 3, 4; cf. Num. 11:26).

In summary, then, we should say that while the 'core' of the Old Testament in the Apostolic Fathers is the same as that accepted among Jews in their time, they are also accustomed to make use of additional apocryphal writings and, more important, to cite them as 'scripture'. At least this is true of the authors of 1–2 Clement and Barnabas, and probably of Hermas as well. Ignatius and Polycarp, responsible to churches less closely related to Judaism and Jewish Christianity, are more careful to quote only from books more widely regarded as canonical. From this fact we can probably infer that in Jewish circles relatively close to Christians the 'canon' was more flexible than it was among those who were opposed both to apocalyptic ideas in general and to Christian ideas in particular. Alternatively, Jewish Christians may have continued to accept books in circulation before the council of Jamnia (e.g., 1 Enoch), as well as similar books written later (e.g., 2 Esdras and 2 Baruch).

Beyond the literature rather widely accepted among Jewish Christians and often treated as authoritative by others, there was a broad spectrum of writings accepted by some Christians and some Gnostics but related to Old Testament revelation. For example, Justin seems to refer to the *Ascension of Isaiah* (*Dial.* 120, 5); and this book was used both by Origen and by the Archontic Gnostics. Most popular of all was 1 Enoch, used by the secretaries at Qumran, by Jude, Barnabas, Athenagoras, and Irenaeus, later by Tertullian and Origen, as well as by several authors of Gnostic apocalypses. Jews and Christians alike made use of various *Testaments of the Patriarchs*.

Christians who were fairly closely in touch with rabbinical Judaism, however, were aware that books like these were not accepted by most Jews, and in the case of Origen we can see that when he moved from Alexandria to Caesarea in Palestine he became somewhat more cautious in his usage of these books, especially in regard to 1 Enoch.[1]

The use of Greek versions

In the course of the second century, as Christians continued to make use of books not accepted by most Jews, and continued to use the Greek translation which Jews were beginning to reject, it was necessary to establish a theoretical

[1] See R. P. C. Hanson, *Origen's Doctrine of Tradition* (London, 1954), 136.

foundation for these practices. (1) Because Christians, as early as the time of Barnabas, made use of 2 Esdras, it was possible to rely upon the statement that by divine inspiration Ezra had restored the Old Testament scriptures, burned in the time of the Exile, and—though the Christian writers do not say so—added seventy more books. This legend first appears in Irenaeus (*Adv. haer.* 3, 21, 2) and is repeated by Tertullian, Clement, and Origen; Eusebius (*H. E.* 5, 8, 15) copies it from Irenaeus. (2) The origin of the Septuagint had been described, about 100 B.C., in the *Letter of Aristeas*, and Philo of Alexandria had provided an analogous account while insisting upon the divine inspiration of the translators (*Vit. Mos.* 2, 25–44). Josephus (*Ant.* 12, 12–118) copied and revised the account given in the *Letter*.[1] Among Christians, even more than among Hellenistic Jews, the authenticity and inspiration of the Septuagint required defence, and we find the legend recurring in Justin (*Apol.* 1, 31), Irenaeus (*Adv. haer.* 3, 21, 2), Clement, Tertullian and Julius Africanus. Eusebius provides very extensive quotations from the *Letter of Aristeas*.[2]

Beyond the question of inspiration and authenticity lay that of text. The latter question is first discussed, as we should expect, in Justin's *Dialogue with Trypho*, an exposition of the prophetic meaning of the Old Testament. Justin claims that many passages which point toward Christ have been deleted from the Greek Old Testament as read by Jews (*Dial.* 71–73, 120, 124, 137–38). Some of these passages may be based on early variants in the Septuagint text, but most of them actually look like Christian additions.

In *Dialogue* 71–72 Justin lists the three most important passages. The first is a rather obscure paragraph supposedly

---

1 A. Pelletier, *Flavius Josèphe, adaptateur de la Lettre d'Aristée* (Paris, 1962).

2 Pelletier, *Lettre d'Aristée à Philocrate* (Paris, 1962), 22–41.

from 1 Esdras. 'And Esdras said to the people, "This Passover is our Savior and our refuge; and if you understand, and it enters into your heart, that we are going to humiliate him in a sign, and afterwards we may set our hope on him, this place will never be laid waste, says the God of the Powers; but if you do not believe him or listen to his preaching, you will be an object of ridicule to the gentiles."' The idea that Christ is the Christians' Passover is set forth by Paul in 1 Corinthians 5:7, on which the author of this interpolation may well have relied.[1] Clement of Alexandria may know it; he speaks of Esdras as instituting 'the saving Passover' (*Str.* 1, 124, 2).[2]

The second is supposed to come from Jeremiah. 'The Lord God, the Holy One [emending the text from Irenaeus] of Israel, remembered his dead who slept in the earth of burial, and he descended to them to proclaim his act of salvation to them.' With minor variants, Irenaeus quotes this text five times and paraphrases it once;[3] the fact that he ascribes it twice to Jeremiah, once to Isaiah, and once to 'the prophet' suggests that he is using an anthology—which may well have included the passage from Esdras as well, since they are on similar subjects.

The third is found at the end of Psalm 95 (quoted in *Dialogue* 73) or in the parallel passage 1 Chronicles 16: 23-31 (quoted in *Apology* 41, 4). To the words 'The Lord reigned' was added the phrase 'from the tree', i.e., the cross. The interpolation is probably earlier than the Epistle of Barnabas, in which it seems to be noticed (8:5).[4]

1 The passage recurs, perhaps from Justin, in Lactantius, *Div. inst.* 4, 18, 22.

2 On 'the saving Passover' see B. Lohse, *Das Passafest der Quartadecimaner* (Gütersloh, 1953), 50–56.

3 *Adv. haer.* 3, 20, 4; 4, 22, 1. 33, 1. 33, 12; 5, 31, 1; *Epid.* 78.

4 See P. Prigent, *L'Epître de Barnabé I–XVI et ses sources* (Paris, 1961), 113.

These passages, along with the refusal of Trypho, Justin's Jewish opponent, to accept them, show that in the middle of the second century the Old Testament canon as accepted by Christians was beginning to be somewhat different from the canon accepted by Jews. The difference was accentuated because of (1) the continuing Christian use of the Septuagint in various forms, (2) the continuing Christian use of Old Testament anthologies with garbled or interpolated texts, and (3) the rise of new Greek translations among Jews.

The first witness we have to such translations is, once more, Justin, who says to Trypho that 'you and your teachers venture to say that in the prophecy of Isaiah [7:14] it is not said "Behold the virgin will conceive" but "Behold the young woman will conceive and bear a son" ' (*Dial.* 43, 8, etc.). The next witness, Irenaeus (*Adv. haer.* 3, 21, 1), goes on to give a little information about two translators, Aquila of Pontus and Theodotion of Ephesus, both of whom he calls proselytes to Judaism. According to rabbinic tradition Aquila was a disciple of Rabbi Akiba, about A.D. 130. The existence of these translations, and of the one made a few years later by Symmachus, must have encouraged Christians both to insist upon the importance of the Septuagint and to adhere to its text fairly closely.

If we try to discover some pattern in the ideas of the Old Testament canon as reflected in Christian writers of the period between the New Testament and the rise of the school of Alexandria in the third century, we find that in so far as such a pattern exists it is caused by contact with Jews and their ideas of canonical Hebrew books. Generally speaking, however, Christians did not hold any clear ideas about the limits of their own Old Testament. It included books of wisdom and piety not found in the Hebrew canon; it also included some books derived from the Jewish apocalyptic movement.

Probably the best way to explain the situation and its results is by using the words of A. C. Sundberg, Jr.: 'the canon of the Old Testament took its form in the church as the resultant between the forces of Christian usage that tended to maintain a book as canonical in the church and the *a priori* claims of the Jewish canon that tended to restrict the Christian Old Testament to the limits of the Jewish definition of scripture.'[1]

This means that while Christians who were concerned with defining a New Testament canon analogous to the Old Testament collection could claim that there was such an entity as an Old Testament canon, they were in no position, at least in the first few centuries, to say exactly what was in it. The Old Testament canon during this time was more a process than an achievement. We shall see that a similar observation can be made in regard to the New Testament.

1 *Harvard Theological Review* 51 (1958), 226.

III

Books and traditions

If we look only at the Old Testament when we are considering the formation of the New we are likely to envisage early Christianity as a movement more literary-minded and, indeed, more definitely fixed than it actually was. Christianity actually arose in an environment in which oral traditions were flourishing—that is to say, within Palestinian Judaism. Proof that such traditions were constantly in circulation is provided not only by references in the writings of Philo and Josephus[1] and in later rabbinic writings but also by statements made in the New Testament itself, primarily in the synoptic gospels.

Especially from Mark 7:1–13 it is clear that oral tradition was a living power among Jesus' contemporaries (cf. Matt. 15:1–3, 7–9). Pharisees and others criticize Jesus' disciples for eating with unwashed hands and not maintaining 'the tradition of the elders'. In his reply to them he quotes Isaiah's contrast between worship with lips and worship with the heart; the former is identified with 'human' tradition, and Jesus goes on to contrast it with 'the word of God', which they are rejecting. In Matthew 23 there is a whole series of examples of Pharisaic tradition, apparently criti-

1 Philo *ap*. Eusebius, *Praep. Ev.* 8, 7, 6; Josephus, *Ant.* 13, 297, 408.

cized on the ground not that it is invalid but that it is not all-important.

When Paul says that he was once 'in regard to the law, a Pharisee' (Phil. 3:5) he means, as the parallel in Galatians 1:14 shows, that he was 'exceedingly zealous for the traditions of my fathers'—i.e. the Jewish sages whose sayings are recorded in a treatise like *Pirke Aboth*. In other words, he was well acquainted with the Jewish conception of tradition—one which, as a Christian, he continued to employ.

Not only Paul, however, but other Christians as well regarded the transmission of the gospel as a process of 'tradition'. The preface to Luke's gospel contains a description of 'many' who have tried to compose literary accounts of the events and have relied upon what was handed down by 'those who from the beginning were eye-witnesses and servants of the matter' (1:3); he himself is relying on similar sources.

The synoptic gospels (Matthew, Mark, and Luke) are almost certainly based upon oral traditions, arranged partly by the evangelists and partly by their predecessors, and often tied together by verbal association. We must beware, however, of making too much of this point. In the 'moment' of writing something that he remembers, a writer will almost necessarily rely on association of some sort, and it is often difficult to decide whether he is relying on something he himself is arranging, or has previously arranged, or on something others have transmitted to him. No matter what conclusion we reach on this point, however, the ways in which various kinds of words of Jesus and stories about him are preserved in the synoptic gospels strongly suggest that a process of oral transmission lies behind them. (To some extent this situation is also characteristic of the Gospel of John.)[1]

1 Cf. C. H. Dodd, *Historical Tradition in the Fourth Gospel* (Cambridge, 1963).

For more precise information we must turn to the earlier Pauline epistles. When Paul wrote to the Christians of Corinth in southern Greece about the year 54 he reminded them of a tradition which he had received (ultimately) from the Lord and had previously delivered to them. This traditional account told of how 'the Lord Jesus, in the night when he was betrayed, took bread; and when he had given thanks he broke it and said, "Take, eat; this is my body which is broken for you; do this in remembrance of me" '. The story continues with a statement about the eucharistic cup. 'Likewise, after supper he took the cup, saying, "This cup is the new covenant in my blood; do this, as often as you drink it, in remembrance of me"' (1 Cor. 11:23–25).

Paul's words do not show that the Christians were accustomed to recite these words at their celebrations of the Lord's Supper. They do show that a traditional account of the Last Supper was available to them, and that this account was set in a context of the Lord's betrayal and death, with some chronological detail ('the night when he was betrayed'). Furthermore, the story, whether recited at the Eucharist or not, was clearly eucharistic in purpose ('do this').

This bit of tradition therefore shows two things: first, it comes from a narrative at least partly continuous; and second, it has acquired, either from the beginning or in the course of transmission, a definite liturgical reference. It is concerned with what Jesus did and said—in relation to the life of the Church.

Another significant tradition or group of traditions is to be found in 1 Corinthians 15:3–7. Here Paul speaks again of what he had received and had delivered. It consists of two parts, the first about Jesus' death and resurrection, the second about those to whom he appeared after the resurrection. The first is as follows:

Christ died
> for our sins
>> in accordance with the scriptures;

he was buried;
he was raised
> on the third day
>> in accordance with the scriptures.

Here we obviously encounter a semi-credal formula not unlike what we later find in the developed creeds of the Church. Since Paul says that he received it from tradition, it is clear that before his time the leaders of the Church, probably at Jerusalem, had already developed explanations—indeed, authoritative explanations—of the death and resurrection of Christ. Why did Christ die? For our sins, and 'in accordance with the scriptures'; presumably the primary Old Testament text in view was Isaiah 53:6–12, which discusses the relation of the Suffering Servant's death to the sins of others. It may be that the clause 'he was buried' was interpreted in the same way Isaiah 53:9 says that 'he made his grave with the wicked'. The last clause undoubtedly refers to the tradition of Christ's resurrection on the third day (Sunday after Friday), and the Old Testament text is probably Hosea 6:2: 'After two days he will revive us; on the third day he will raise us up, and we shall live in his sight.'

This is to say that the tradition which Paul is transmitting is not a simple 'factual' account, although facts are undoubtedly involved; it is a factual account interpreted theologically with reference to the plan of God as revealed by the prophets.

With this tradition Paul combines another about the witnesses to the resurrection. He probably knows two groups of witnesses, the one headed by Cephas (Peter), the other by James. The first group consists of Cephas, the Twelve, and more than 500 Christians, most of whom are still alive. The second includes James, 'all the apostles', and —perhaps—Paul himself. These lists can be examined from various points of view. First of all, we should say that Paul is trying to present a complete list. On this basis, it is strange that he says nothing about Mary Magdalene (John 20:14–18; Mark 16:9) and that he includes an appearance to James which we find described only in the apocryphal *Gospel of the Hebrews*. But perhaps it is more important to ask why he has what he has. Both lists are headed by names of the principal apostles whom he encountered when he went up to Jerusalem for what he says was his first visit as a Christian, about the year 35: Peter and James the Lord's brother (Gal. 1:18–19). We can hardly suppose that at that point they refrained from speaking of the resurrection to him. The simplest explanation of the origin of the tradition is that it was transmitted to him by Peter and James, and that Peter spoke of himself, the Twelve, and the 500 Christians, while James spoke of himself and 'all the apostles'—since he was not one of the Twelve but had come to be regarded as an apostle. It was natural for Paul to ally himself with the latter tradition because, like James, he had not been an early disciple of Jesus. We may well suppose, then, that Paul arranged the tradition as we find it so that it would end with James, 'all the apostles' (probably James and the others at Jerusalem), and himself. No less than Paul, James was added to the earliest group; no less than Paul, James later became an apostle.

The tradition about the witnesses to the resurrection, then, while based upon the evidence of eye-witnesses ('he appeared' or 'he was seen'), contains some traces of purposeful editing. It does not present a simple account of 'what actually happened'; it combines such an account with motives which we probably can identify in Paul's case but can only surmise in the case of others.

In the earlier Pauline epistles we also encounter traditions which report what Jesus said, apart from any historical context. For example, in 1 Thessalonians 4:15–18 Paul justifies his statement that living Christians will not go before those who have died by appealing to a 'word of the Lord'. (His point may conceivably be related to the saying preserved in Mark 9:1: 'There are some of those who stand here who will not taste death until they have seen the kingdom of God come with power.') The 'word of the Lord' to which he refers is this: 'The Lord himself will come down from heaven with a shout, with the voice of the archangel, and with the trumpet of God, and the dead in Christ will rise first; then we who are alive and remain shall be caught up, together with them, in the clouds, to meet the Lord in the air; and thus we shall always be with the Lord.' We conclude that this is the 'word of the Lord' from what Paul adds at the end: 'Encourage one another with these words.' It would appear that this tradition was known in other circles, for many of the details in it are to be found, related to the coming of the Son of Man, in Matthew 24:30–44— the coming of the Son of Man in the clouds of heaven, the angels, the trumpet—as well as the title 'Lord' obviously used of the Son of Man (24:42).

Paul continues his letter by telling the Thessalonians that he has no need to write them about 'times and seasons', for they know that 'the day of the Lord comes like a thief in the night' (5:1–2). Similarly in Matthew 24:42–44 we read that the Lord, or the Son of Man, will come unexpectedly; and his coming is compared with that of a thief.

We conclude that this section of 1 Thessalonians is based on a collection of sayings of Jesus which Paul not only uses for the purpose of exhorting the Thessalonians but also preserves with a high degree of fidelity.

In 1 Corinthians 7:10–11 he discusses the question of the

separation of husbands and wives with reference to a command of the Lord.

> To the married I command—not I, but the Lord—that a wife is not to separate from her husband; if she should separate, she is to remain unmarried or be reconciled to her husband; and a husband is not to divorce his wife.

He is obviously referring to a saying of Jesus preserved in the synoptic gospels (e.g., Mark 10:11–12). The statements are identical: separation is forbidden but tolerated; remarriage is forbidden but not tolerated. Paul goes on to make a clear distinction between the teaching of the Lord and his own inferences based upon it (1 Cor. 7:12): 'to the rest say I, not the Lord'. Clearly, he was quite capable of differentiating the tradition as to what Jesus said from the conclusions he himself drew. And this point is clinched by what he says in 1 Corinthians 7:25, 'Concerning virgins I have no command of the Lord; but I give my judgment as one who has obtained mercy from the Lord to be trustworthy.' He knows the difference between what the Lord said and what he himself is saying.

Another saying of the Lord is attested in 1 Corinthians 9:14, where Paul is speaking of the duty of Christian congregations to provide a living for their ministers. 'The Lord commanded that those who proclaim the gospel should live from the gospel.' Here he almost certainly has in mind the saying recorded in Matthew 10:7 as 'the workman is worthy of his food' and in Luke 10:7 as 'the laborer is worthy of his wage'. It may well be that he has the whole context of the saying in mind, for in Matthew it forms part of a charge to the twelve apostles, and in Luke a charge to 70 (72) disciples.

These examples are not sufficient to show that the Pauline epistles are saturated with reminiscences of sayings of Jesus. They are sufficient, however, to show that Paul certainly knew oral traditions about what Jesus had done and said, and that quite possibly he knew them as arranged in contextual groups. He obviously used them for specific purposes in writing to his churches, but there is no evidence that he distorted them appreciably as he did so. It remains possible that other passages in his letters are based upon traditions of the sayings of Jesus, as Resch, Ropes, and Porter long ago endeavored to show.

Apart from the oral traditions contained in the Pauline letters—probably earlier than any of the written gospels—other traditions of what Jesus said and did were obviously in circulation when, and after, the evangelists wrote. This point is made clear by several verses in the Gospel of John.

> Jesus did many other signs before his disciples which are not recorded in this book (20:30).

> There are many other things which Jesus did; if they were recorded individually I do not think that the world itself would hold the books that would be written (21:25).

In addition, the book of Acts contains a saying of Jesus which is recorded neither in Luke nor in any other gospel: 'remember the words of the Lord Jesus, that he said, "It is more blessed to give than to receive" ' (20:35).

Sayings which occur in the gospels are especially common in the letter of James. Opinions differ as to how many allusions there are; Gerhard Kittel thought there might be 18 or 20,[1] but we are concerned only with claiming that there are at least a few—as there are also in 1 Peter.

This is to say that in the earliest Church there were not only written documents but unwritten traditions, and that the traditions existed before the documents came into

1 *Zeitschrift für die neutestamentliche Wissenschaft* 43 (1950–51), 83–84.

existence. In time the oral traditions faded away, but they continued to circulate not only while the documents were being written but also while the New Testament was being formed.

It is important to recognize that sayings traditionally ascribed to Jesus not only were in circulation at the end of the first century and the beginning of the second but continued to be employed by Christian writers long afterwards. Relatively early, as we shall see (Chapters IV and V), they were appreciatively cited by Jewish Christians like Papias and the author of 2 Clement, and also by Ignatius, relatively remote from Jewish Christianity. They were not confined to any particular group in the early Church, for we encounter them in the writings of Justin, Irenaeus, Clement, and Origen—and later—as well as in Gnostic documents. For instance, the saying 'There shall be schisms and heresies' (which may actually be based on 1 Corinthians 11:18–19) is ascribed to Jesus by Justin (*Dial.* 35, 3), Lactantius, and the author of the fourth-century treatise *De trinitate*; it is also to be found in the *Didascalia Apostolorum* and in the *Clementine Homilies*.[1] Another favorite was 'Seek the great things and the little things will be added for you'. This occurs in Clement of Alexandria, Origen, Eusebius, and Ambrose.[2] 'Become approved moneychangers' was perhaps the most popular. It is found in works of the Marcionite Apelles, Clement, Origen, Dionysius of Alexandria, and later writers, as well as in the *Didascalia* and the *Clementine Homilies*. Some ascribe it to Jesus, others to Paul. Sometimes it is said to come from 'scripture', sometimes from the gospel or the gospels.[3]

1 A. Resch in *Texte und Untersuchungen* 30, 3–4 (Leipzig, 1906), 100–1 (♯ 75).

2 *Ibid.*, 111–12 (♯ 86).

3 *Ibid.*, 112–28 (♯ 87).

The continued use of oral tradition meant that while the determination of a New Testament canon was important it could never be regarded as all-important. Just as among the Jews a measure of freedom was maintained by means of the oral, so among Christians freedom was preserved in the oral tradition. The authority of 'scripture' was upheld, but it was a flexible authority because of the oral tradition and because of the freedom of exegetes to expound both scripture and tradition. Even though leading churchmen almost universally rejected apocryphal gospels and other similar documents, they often continued to accept sayings of Jesus contained in these gospels and not in the others. And even Jerome, with all his leanings toward rigorism, allowed that there might be gold in the 'mud' of the apocryphal gospels.

IV

The witness of the Apostolic Fathers: Jewish Christianity

———

The most important witnesses to the New Testament books as used in the early Church are obviously the writings of the Christians who first wrote after the New Testament writers. These writings are included in the collection known since the seventeenth century (and implicitly so styled a millennium earlier) as 'the Apostolic Fathers'. The writings are highly diverse in form and content; they come from various places under various circumstances and were variously regarded by Christians after their times. They consist of (1) a letter of the Roman church to the Corinthian church, apparently written by a Roman leader named Clement (1 Clement); (2) a sermon probably not by the same author but handed down with 1 Clement (2 Clement); (3) seven letters written from Asia Minor by Ignatius, bishop of Antioch, on his way to martyrdom; (4) a letter to the Philippians by Polycarp, bishop of Smyrna; (5) the account of Polycarp's martyrdom written in the name of the Christians of Smyrna; (6) the fragments of Polycarp's contemporary Papias, bishop (?) of Hierapolis in Phrygia; (7) an epistle ascribed to Paul's fellow-evangelist Barnabas; and (8) the Visions, Mandates, and Similitudes which constitute the *Shepherd* by a Roman Christian named Hermas.

In the nineteenth century there was discovered the *Didache*, or 'teaching of the apostles', a manual of church discipline from the late first century.

Conceivably one could try to arrange these documents in roughly chronological order and then trace the development of the New Testament canon in relation to it. Two factors stand in our way, however. (1) The dates of these writings can be ascertained fairly clearly, but—apart from the *Martyrdom of Polycarp*—all of them were written during a generation, between about A.D. 95 and 125–130. They are too close in time for us to be sure that there was any definite development. (2) Their geographical diversity and, more important, their ideological diversity is such that it would seem better to treat them as representatives of ways of thinking, not of particular periods of time. Christianity, it cannot be said too often, did not develop in a straight line or even along several parallel lines. The only conspicuous 'tendencies' we can find in the early second century are related to the influences of Jewish Christianity and Hellenistic Christianity—although here too we must avoid over-rigid classifications. The Apostolic Fathers who oppose Judaism or Judaizing are often influenced by Jewish ways of thinking; those who might seem to be very Jewish, in turn, make use of Greek rhetoric. Furthermore, to draw a sharp line between 'Jew and Greek' in the early Church is to misunderstand it completely. Converts to Christianity entered a community where such lines had been, and were being, intentionally broken down. In addition, within Jewish circles Greek ideas were flourishing and in Greek circles—if we may take some of the more philosophically minded Gnostics as guides—Jewish ideas were by no means excluded.

In spite of these qualifications, however, we are likely to find that certain attitudes toward the Old Testament and

toward the New Testament books will be more often
expressed by Christians whom we can very broadly treat as
Jewish, while different attitudes will be found among
those farther from Judaism. For this reason we venture to
classify the writings of the Apostolic Fathers in two categories. The first—the more Jewish—will comprise the
Didache, Papias, and the *Shepherd* of Hermas, along with
the 'mixed' writings ascribed to Clement. The second—the
more Hellenistic—will consist of the letters of Ignatius and
Polycarp[1] and the Epistle of Barnabas. The first group will
be discussed in this chapter and the next; the second, in
Chapter VI.

The Didache

The *Didache* begins with five chapters of catechetical
instruction, summarized in the sixth as 'this way of the
teaching'. The five chapters consist of four about the 'way
of life' and one about the 'way of death'. All the allusions
to gospel teaching in the catechetical materials occur in the
first chapter about the way of life, but the passage containing
these allusions is lacking in the Latin version of the *Didache*
and in the paraphrase of it provided in the fifth century by
Schenute of Atripe in Egypt. On the other hand, this passage
(1:3b–2:1) is found in the only complete manuscript of the
Didache and in a fourth-century Greek papyrus fragment,
as well as in two fourth-century manuals based on the
Didache. If it is an interpolation, it is probably an early one.

The passage is presented as an explanation of the basic
way of life, which is to love God and neighbor and not to
do to another what you do not want done to yourself (1:2).
'The teaching of these words is this.'

1 The *Martyrdom of Polycarp* is late and casts practically no light
on the question.

Bless those who curse you and pray for your enemies; fast for those who persecute you. For what credit is it if you love those who love you? Do not the gentiles do the same? But as for you, love those who hate you, and you will have no enemy (1:3).

The words which the Didachist uses are not identical with those found either in Matthew (5:44, 46, 47; 7:12) or in Luke (6:31–33).[1] He is either using oral tradition or quoting from memories of written books; for the moment we shall not try to decide which. More quotations follow almost immediately.

If anyone gives you a blow on the right cheek, turn the other to him too—and you will be perfect. If anyone impresses you to go one mile, go two with him. If anyone takes your coat, give him your shirt too. If anyone takes what is yours away from you, do not ask it back—for you cannot (*Did.* 1:4).

Here the sayings are also found in Matthew (5:39, 48, 41, 40) and Luke (6:30), and again they are presented in such a way that we cannot tell just how the author acquired them.

In the conclusion to the section on the ways (6:1) there seems to be an allusion to Matthew 24:4. 'See that no one makes you err' from this way of teaching. The conclusion suggests that the Didachist is probably using Matthew from memory and supplementing it with other memories of Luke.

The next two chapters (7–8) of the *Didache* are concerned with baptism, fasting, and prayer; in them are very definite quotations from the Gospel of Matthew. (1) Christians are to recite all these things (the teaching of chapters 1–6) and then 'baptize in the name of the Father and of the Son and of the Holy Spirit' (7:1). This looks like an echo of Matthew 28:19, where the disciples are told to make disciples of (or

---

1 For early Christian use of this teaching see the Appended Note to Chapter IX.

C

teach) all the nations and baptize them 'in the name of the Father and of the Son and of the Holy Spirit'. (2) Christians are not to fast with the 'hypocrites'; here the Didachist is expounding the doctrine of Matthew 6:16. (3) Finally, they are not to pray as the hypocrites do (Matt. 6:5), but 'as the Lord commanded in his Gospel' (8:2).

> Our Father, who art in heaven, hallowed be thy name; thy kingdom come; thy will be done on earth as it is in heaven. Give us this day our daily bread, and forgive us our debt as we forgive our debtors, and lead us not into temptation, but deliver us from evil, for thine is the power and the glory forever.

This can hardly be anything but the prayer recorded in Matthew 6:9–13. The presence of the doxology (in this form also in the Sahidic New Testament) does not prove that the Didachist is making use of liturgical memories instead of a gospel, for the gospel he used may already have received liturgical enrichment.

In the eucharistic prayers (9–10) there seem to be echoes of the eucharistic passage in the Gospel of John (chapter 6) and of the 'Lord's prayer' in John 17; but they are not sufficiently precise for us to claim that the Didachist knew John. They may reflect a tradition common to him and the Fourth Evangelist. An explicit quotation, however, occurs in *Didache* 9:5: 'the Lord said, "Do not give the holy thing to the dogs" ' (Matt. 7:6).

Again, in the discussion of the ministry which follows (11–13) there is a clear allusion to Matthew 12:31: 'every sin will be forgiven, but this sin [against the Holy Spirit] will not be forgiven' (*Did.* 11:7). And at the end of the whole 'practical' section (15:3–4) more echoes are to be found.

> Do not reprove one another in wrath, but in peace, as you have it in the gospel, and let no one speak to anyone who wrongs his

neighbor, nor let that one be heard among you until he repents. But perform your prayers and alms and all your actions as you have it in the gospel of our Lord.

These words, in part recapitulating what has been said before (e.g., *Did.* 14:1–2), contain no direct quotations from 'the gospel' but sum up the teaching of Matthew 5:22–26 and 18:15–35.

Whether or not the last chapter of the *Didache* (16), a little apocalypse, was originally a part of the document, it is clearly based upon a similar apocalypse in Matthew 24.

We conclude, therefore, that while it is possible that some of what the Didachist quoted from or alluded to may be oral tradition, it is highly probable that he knew the Gospel of Matthew and that when he spoke of what Christians 'have in the gospel' or 'have in the gospel of our Lord' he was referring to this book. The presence of passages in the first part of the *Didache* which seem closer to Luke than to Matthew may be due to the Didachist's inexact quotations from memory.

The primary authorities for the Didachist do not seem to be written books, however, but 'the commandments of the Lord', to which nothing is to be added and from which nothing is to be taken away (4:13). These commandments are certainly expressed in the gospel tradition, whether oral or written; from this the Didachist derives the 'law of love' (1:2; cf. Matt. 22:37–39 and parallels) and its explanation, his statement that 'the meek will inherit the earth' (3:7; Matt. 5:5), and the injunctions about baptism, fasting, prayer (7–8), and reconciliation (14:2), as well as the eschatological materials of chapter 16.[1] The commandments are also anticipated in the Old Testament, including not only 'ancient prophets' (11:11) like Malachi (cited in 14:3) and

1 See also 1:5: 'he will not come out from there until he pays the last *quadrans*'—based on Matt. 5:26.

Zechariah (cited in 16:7) but also later Jewish writings like Sirach (cited in 1:6).[1]

The very close relationship of the Didachist to the Gospel of Matthew suggests that he may have been acquainted with it as a written document, although it may be, as J.-P. Audet has suggested,[2] that he used it thus only in the last six chapters of his work, earlier relying on oral tradition. His teaching about apostles and prophets 'in accordance with the decree of the gospel' (11:3) would thus be based on Matthaean passages, as would his injunction to 'perform your prayers and alms and all your actions as you have it in the gospel of our Lord' (15:4).

Our information, however, permits us to say very little about the Didachist's views of scripture (a term he never employs), especially in regard to a New Testament. There are commandments to which nothing can be added and from which nothing can be taken away, but since he adds the negative form of the Golden Rule to the 'law of love' (1:2) and does not hesitate to paraphrase the Decalogue (2:2–3), he can hardly have regarded books as his primary authorities, although he does quote what was *said* both by the Old Testament prophets and others and by the Lord. His primary authority, then, must be tradition, whether oral or written. The freedom with which he usually treats the tradition reminds us of that found in Jewish schools of his time—and in Christian schools as well.

Papias of Hierapolis

Another witness to the continued exaltation of tradition in Jewish Christian circles is Papias of Hierapolis in Phrygia—

1 On the form of the quotation see C. H. Turner in *Journal of Theological Studies* 7 (1905–06), 593–95.

2 *La Didaché: instructions des apôtres* (Paris, 1958), 104–20.

according to late tradition, perhaps based on conjecture, bishop there—who was a contemporary of Polycarp and probably flourished early in the second century. He wrote five books of *Exegeses of the Dominical Oracles*, a title which probably refers to Old Testament predictions and prefigurations although, since most of the work has disappeared, we cannot be sure that this is correct. The seventh-century writer Anastasius of Sinai tells us that he referred the creation story to Christ and the Church and the story of paradise to the Church. If Anastasius was right (and we have no reason to question his statement), Papias obviously regarded Genesis, and along with it the rest of the Old Testament, as sacred scripture containing prefigurations of the gospel.

In the preface to his *Exegeses* (quoted by Eusebius, *H. E.* 3, 39, 3–4) he stated that he was concerned not with the quantity of the tradition he could obtain but with its quality as derived from the Lord. In addition, he valued oral tradition much more highly than what was written in books. This tradition came from 'a living and continuing voice', which Papias evidently regarded as free from error. For this reason he made an effort to find out about the oral teaching of the elders or disciples of the Lord, such as Andrew, Peter, Philip, Thomas, James, John (these names occur in the Gospel of John, in this order), and Matthew. He wanted to find out what these disciples *said* and what 'Aristion and the elder John, disciples of the Lord, *are saying*'. He thus differentiated men of the past and men still alive—and he clearly was acquainted with two men named John, one an apostle (though Papias does not use the title), the other an elder. His statement suggests that books containing traditions derived at least from John and Matthew are in existence, but he wants to go behind books to tradition. According to Eusebius, Papias frequently mentioned his living informants by name.

The value of the traditions he thus acquired has been assessed differently by various authors. Eusebius was most unenthusiastic about them. They included a miracle story about the daughters of Philip (the evangelist of Acts 21:8, whom Papias—or Eusebius—may have identified with the apostle), a contemporary resurrection account, a tale about Justus Barsabbas' safely drinking poison (cf. Acts 1:23), some 'strange parables and instructions of the Savior', and other rather mythical materials. What Eusebius especially disliked was the notion that there would be a thousand-year period on earth after the resurrection from the dead (Rev. 20:4–6); he suggested that Papias took literally what the apostles meant figuratively. Irenaeus, on the other hand, did not hesitate to quote Papias for what the Lord had said about the miraculous fertility of the earth in the days to come. In this future golden age there would be vines each one of which would produce grapes 10,000 to the fifth power; and each grape would give 25 measures of wine—apparently about 225 gallons! 'And when one of the saints takes a cluster, another cluster will cry out, "I am better; take me; bless the Lord through me!"' All the rest of the vegetable creation would be similarly productive, and the animals would become herbivorous, peaceable, and subject to mankind. According to Papias, the traitor Judas expressed his doubts about this prediction, but the Lord replied, 'Those who come in that day will behold'.[1]

The singular feature of the quotation is that, although in Papias' narrative the prediction has been given a framework which includes a discussion between Jesus and Judas Iscariot, it actually consists of an almost exact transcription of the Jewish apocalypse known as 2 Baruch (29:6). Perhaps this is not a complete surprise; we have seen that

[1] Irenaeus, *Adv. haer.* 5, 33, 3–4. According to Papias, the prophecy came to him from John the Lord's disciple.

the author of Barnabas regarded 2 Baruch as the work of a prophet; but he did not ascribe Baruch's words to Jesus. Papias' words suggest that his zeal for oral tradition was rather excessive.

When we turn to the written books with which he was acquainted, we should suggest—as we have already intimated—that he knew the Gospel of John; he also refers to Christ as 'the Truth' (cf. John 14:6). He explicitly refers to books composed by Mark and Matthew. In discussing Mark he states (following 'the elder') that the evangelist, Peter's interpreter, wrote down accurately and completely what Peter taught about the Lord's sayings and doings—but not 'in order' (either rhetorical or chronological). Apparently Mark's order has been criticized, presumably in relation to the Gospel of John.[1] As for Matthew, he 'composed the oracles in a [the?] Hebrew dialect, but each translated them as he was able'. This enigmatic sentence (1) refers not to sayings of Jesus (*logoi*) but to Old Testament predictions (*logia*), and (2) suggests that various Greek writings similar to one another and probably ascribed to Matthew are in circulation.[2] Papias does not want to decide which one is the most reliable. He treats all as translations, just as he treats Mark as a translation of Peter's teaching.

This information shows that Papias knew the gospels of Mark and Matthew and it also suggests that he did not regard them as scripture. His matter-of-fact discussions contains nothing about the inspiration of the evangelists. A story about the death of Judas, relayed by Apollinarius of Laodicea in the late fourth century, may be intended to supplement the story of his death in Acts, but this is highly uncertain.

1 Since the arrangement of Mark is close to that of Matthew and Luke.
2 One may be the Gospel of the Hebrews; see below.

According to Eusebius (*H. E.* 3, 39, 17), Papias also made use of 1 John and 1 Peter, and told a story about a woman 'accused of many sins before the Lord' which was in the apocryphal *Gospel of the Hebrews*. It is sometimes suggested that this is the story now found in John 7:53–8:11, but the woman there described was accused not of many sins but of one. Later Christian writers tell us that Papias regarded the Revelation of John as 'trustworthy', presumably meaning 'inspired'.

What we find in Papias, then, is a combination of three or more written gospels (Matthew=Hebrews [?], Mark, and John) with a mass of Jewish-Christian oral traditions and, in additon, 1 John and 1 Peter. There is no trace of the Pauline epistles, and these epistles may be the writings which Papias regards as least acceptable. When he says that unlike 'the many' he does not take pleasure in those who say a great deal, he may have Paul in mind. Following Eusebius' lead we may suggest that if Papias read the Pauline letters he probably could not, or would not, understand them (cf. 2 Peter 3:16).

Papias' limited 'New Testament' is significant only in its reflection of usage in a rather backward community, where devotion to oral tradition prevented the development of a clear idea of canonicity. Indeed, to ascribe a New Testament canon of any sort to Papias would be a mistake. Just as for contemporary Jewish exegetes, the only written authority for him is the Old Testament. With it there is another authority, the oral Law—for Papias expressed in the Christian traditions.

Hermas of Rome

Another representative of Jewish Christianity in the early second century is Hermas, who wrote his *Shepherd* at Rome perhaps between 90 and 120 or so—unless, as S. Giet has recently argued,[1] the work was produced by three different writers. Since the dates which Giet assigns to his authors are rather tentative, and since all the authors reflect Jewish Christian ideas current at Rome, we shall not go into the question of authorship—although all the positive evidence for Hermas' knowledge of New Testament books comes from the 9th Similitude, assigned by Giet to Hermas II.

As a whole the *Shepherd* is full of allusions to Old Testament phrases, and its apocalyptic framework seems to be based upon that of 2 Esdras. In Mand. 4, 3, 1 Hermas (or Hermas III) says that he has 'heard from some teachers that there is no second repentance beyond the one given when we went down into the water and received remission of our former sins'. The teachers may well have been relying on Hebrews (6:4–6)—a book, as we have seen, well known to Clement of Rome—but Hermas probably does not know the book.

It is in the 9th Similitude that we find clear teaching about entering into the kingdom of God by receiving the Name of the Son of God (9, 12)—teaching which seems to reflect John 3:3, 5. Hermas identifies the Name of the Son with the person of the Son and with a 'gate' to the kingdom. With this identification we may compare John 10:7–9 (Christ is the door; he who enters through him will be saved) and 14:6 (no one comes to the Father but through me).

Teaching about the kingdom of God from the synoptics is reflected in Similitude 9, 20. There we read about thorns as those involved in business and about business men as choked by their work. Hermas has become confused by his memories of the parable of the sower (Mark 4:7; Matt. 13:7) and its explanation (Mark 4:18–19; Matt. 13:22); he finally achieves clarity when he recalls the definite statement

1 *Hermas et les Pasteurs* (Paris, 1963).

of Mark 10:23 (cf. Matt. 19:23) about the difficulty with which the rich will enter into the kingdom of God.

Finally (Sim. 9, 29, 30) he deals with another gospel statement about entering the kingdom, this time from Matthew 18:3: 'Unless you turn and become like the children you will not enter into the kingdom of heaven.' Christians must be 'like children' living free from wickedness in a state of innocence. Hermas seems to be combining the gospel saying with something like the word of Paul in I Corinthians 14:20.[1]

He may or may not know I Corinthians, but it is almost certain that he knows Ephesians. In Similitude 9, 13 he twice speaks of Christians as becoming or possessing 'one spirit and one body' (Eph. 4:4); in Similitude 9, 17, 3 he says that baptized Christians have 'one understanding and one mind, and their faith became one and their love one'; similarly in Similitude 9, 18, 4 the purified Church will be 'one body, one understanding, one mind, one faith, one love'—and these passages closely resemble Ephesians 4:3–6.

Since the only book to which Hermas explicitly refers is the Jewish apocalypse known as the *Book of Eldad and Modat* (Vis. 2, 3, 4), it is not surprising that New Testament quotations or allusions are so scarce. Indeed, it is rather remarkable that in a Jewish Christian context we find allusions to Ephesians, although at Rome Christians undoubtedly possessed not only gospels but also Pauline epistles (see below, on 1–2 Clement). That Hermas regarded these documents as scripture is most unlikely. The only inspired works to which he refers are *Eldad and Modat* and the little book which he was given in a vision and told to copy (Vis. 2). Since, however, he describes Eldad and Modat as 'having prophesied to the people in the wilderness' it

1 See 'Like Children', *Harvard Theological Review* 39 (1946), 71–73; also Papias, frag. 8 Bihlmeyer.

would appear that he was acquainted with the Old Testament (Num. 11:26). But his fondness for apocalyptic thought and literature takes him far beyond any concern for ideas of canonicity.

In his discussion of the little book revealed to him, however, we find at least the seed of such ideas. Hermas is to make the words of his copy of the book known 'to all the elect'—but he is to do so through the constituted authorities of the Roman church. One copy of the book is to be transmitted through Clement 'to the cities outside, for this is his function'; the other is to be used by Grapte for exhorting the widows and orphans; but Hermas himself is to read the book with 'the presbyters who govern the church' (Vis. 2, 4, 3). To be sure, the primary test of prophetic authenticity is provided by the life and deeds of the prophet (Mand. 11), but Hermas recognizes the importance of 'the apostles and bishops and teachers and deacons . . . who always agreed among themselves and had peace among themselves and listened to one another' (Vis. 3, 5, 1).

It would appear, then, that if Hermas had a canon (as he does not) it would be one recognized as such by these bishops, teachers, and deacons, or the presbyters who govern the church. To say this, however, is not to say that we have any clear idea as to what would have been in it. If it included Matthew and Ephesians it doubtless included other Pauline epistles and perhaps other gospels.

In general, however, it is clear that for Jewish Christians of the first and second centuries the Bible consisted of the Old Testament and some Jewish apocryphal literature. This was their primary written authority. Along with it went traditions, chiefly oral, about the sayings of Jesus. Anything else was secondary; the written gospels were not usually regarded as authoritative writings. What counted was their content as reflecting tradition.

Beyond these witnesses to Jewish Christianity in the early second century lie the views of those whom Ignatius of Antioch regards as 'Judaizers'. These Christians, whose views he discusses most fully in his letter to the Philadelphians, similarly insisted upon the primacy of the Old Testament as a written authority. It will be most convenient, however, to consider their views along with those of Ignatius himself (Chapter VI).

V

The witness of the Apostolic Fathers:
Hellenistic-Jewish Christianity

It is easy enough to classify the *Didache*, Papias, and Hermas together. All alike stand close to Judaism and reflect a
strong continuity with Jewish ideas of the Old Testament
and apocalyptic literature; all lay emphasis on tradition
rather than the books of what was to be the New Testament.

The situation is harder to deal with when we turn to two
documents of the Roman church—Roman, but quite remote
from Hermas—at the end of the first century and the beginning of the second. The first of these, and by all odds the
more important of the two, is the letter from 'the church of
God which sojourns at Rome to the church of God which
sojourns at Corinth', apparently written toward the end of
the last decade of the first century. To be sure, the author of
the letter is not named as Clement until we reach the last
third of the second century; but this fact proves nothing,
since there is very little Christian literature in existence from
an earlier period, and it is fairly obvious that churches as such
do not write letters; individuals write them in the church's
name. We shall refer to the author of the letter as Clement.

His primary authority is the Old Testament, to which he
refers as 'God's oracles' (19:1) or 'sacred scriptures' (53:1).
It is fairly clear that in many instances he has looked up the

passages which he quotes, word for word, from the Greek Bible. It is also possible, however, that he has made use of one or more anthologies in which Old Testament passages had already been combined before his time. Such passages are probably to be found where he runs citations together or locates passages rather vaguely as 'somewhere'. Of course he may be quoting from memory; but the combination of exactness and rather wild inexactness may perhaps be best explained as due to his use of various sources.[1]

If this is, or may be, the case with Clement's use of the Old Testament, it is easier to understand the way in which he makes use of some passages parallel to the gospel tradition. Here there is an important passage in which he urges Christians to 'do what is written' (13:1). By 'what is written' he apparently has in mind primarily the Old Testament examples of 'faith and hospitality' or 'hospitality and piety' which he has just provided in his letter; but he goes on to explain what the Holy Spirit says—in Jeremiah 9: 23–24. 'Let not the wise man boast of his wisdom, or the strong man of his strength, or the rich man of his riches; but he who boasts, let him boast of the Lord, to seek him out and do judgment and righteousness.' An interesting feature of this quotation is that the words 'Let him boast of the Lord' are found not in our text of the Greek Old Testament but in Paul's quotations from it in 1 Corinthians 1:31 and 2 Corinthians 10:17. Conceivably Clement mixed up the quotations from Jeremiah and from Paul; more probably he was using an Old Testament text like Paul's—perhaps an anthology. He then continues with the sentence interrupted by the words about the Holy Spirit and the quotation from Jeremiah. 'Let us do what is written . . . especially remembering the words of the Lord Jesus, which he spoke when

1 On this point cf. R. M. Grant–H. H. Graham, *The Apostolic Fathers* II (New York, 1965), 10–13.

he was teaching gentleness and patience' (13:1, at the end). The structure of the sentence clearly suggests that the words of Jesus (introduced by the formula found in Acts 20:35 and repeated in I Clement 46:7) are included ('especially') in what is written. Christians are to 'walk in obedience to his holy words, in humility, for the holy Word says, "On whom shall I look but on the meek and gentle and him who trembles at my oracles" ' (13:3–4). Here is something of a problem. The word 'word' or 'words' occurs so often that it is hard to tell just what is meant. But it would seem that the most natural explanation of the passages is that all the 'words' in question come from written documents; the last is from Isaiah 66:2, quoted rather freely.

But what were the words of the Lord Jesus? According to Clement, he spoke thus:

Be merciful,/so that/you may obtain mercy;
forgive,/so that/it may be forgiven you;
as you do,/thus/it will be done to you;
as you give,/thus/it will be given to you;
as you judge,/thus/you will be judged;
as you are kind,/thus/kindness will be shown you;
with the measure you measure,/by it/it will be measured to
   you.

These sayings are ultimately based on something much like what we find in various verses of Matthew (5:7, 6:14–15, 7:1–2, 12) and Luke (6:31, 36–38). But they are certainly not derived directly from Matthew or Luke, or even a combination of the two. The structure present in Clement's formulation suggests that he is following some source—not unlike the Old Testament anthology he may have used—already composed for instruction or liturgical usage or both.[1]

1 Cf. H. Koester, *Synoptische Überlieferungen bei den Apostolischen Vätern* (Berlin, 1957), 13–16.

It might be that Clement's reference to the Corinthians as having stored up Christ's words in their hearts and keeping his sufferings before their eyes (2:1) would imply that they relied on oral tradition. But since the sufferings were only figuratively before their eyes (cf. Gal. 3:1) unless they were reading about them, and since it is perfectly possible to remember what one has read in a book, it would appear that their knowledge of Christ's words and deeds could have come through reading as well as through listening.

There is another passage in 1 Clement in which Christians are called to 'remember the words of the Lord Jesus' (46:7–8). The passage begins with a quotation from some apocryphal book (46:2),[1] continues with Psalm 17:26, and proceeds with definite allusions to Ephesians 4:4–6 and Romans 12:5. Then come the words of Jesus.

> Woe to that man: it were good for him if he had not been born rather than to offend one of my elect; it were better for him to be girded with a millstone and to be drowned in the sea than to pervert one of my elect.

These words contain echoes of Matthew (18:6, 26:24) and Luke (17:2, 22:22). Perhaps the verses were brought together in part, by verbal similarity. But we do not know whether the bringing together was done by Clement on this occasion or some earlier one, or by some predecessor. In view of what we have already seen in the letter, it seems likely that he is quoting from a gospel-like book but perhaps not from our written gospels.

From Clement, then, we seem to see that at Rome in his time there was a book of the teaching of Jesus, perhaps including an account of his sufferings (death, and therefore resurrection). This book was obviously much like our

1 See also Hermas, Vis. 3, 6, 2 (AL 1); Sim. 8, 8, 1.

gospels, especially Matthew and Luke, but cannot be precisely identified with them.

Clement's testimony about the Pauline epistles is more definite. He indubitably knows 1 Corinthians, for he writes to the Corinthians as follows:

> Take up the epistle of the blessed Paul the apostle. What did he first write you at 'the beginning of the gospel' [Phil. 4:15]? With true spiritual insight he wrote you about himself and Cephas and Apollos, because even then you had made yourselves partisans [1 Cor. 1:12, 3:22] (47:1–3).

In addition, there are five quite definite allusions to the first four chapters of 1 Corinthians in other passages in 1 Clement as well as five to chapter 12, a paraphrase of 13:4–7, and three to chapter 15. Fewer allusions, eleven in all, are made to Romans, but one of them is especially significant. 1 Clement 35:5–6 contains a paraphrase of Romans 1:29–32; then the author continues, 'For the scripture says'—and a quotation from Psalm 49 (50) follows. This definitely implies that for Clement the Pauline epistles are not scripture, though they are obviously authoritative. It is fairly clear that he also knows Galatians, Philippians and Ephesians, probably also James and 1 Peter.

It is important to observe that in 1 Clement we find the earliest definite allusions to the Epistle to the Hebrews. These occur throughout the first half of the letter and reach a climax in the 36th chapter, which consists almost entirely of echoes from Hebrews; thereafter there are no such allusions.

Morton Smith[1] and others have argued that Clement's account of Peter and Paul in the 5th chapter is chiefly based on the book of Acts, and it may be added that 1 Clement 2:1 contains an allusion to the saying of Jesus found in

1 *New Testament Studies* 7 (1960–61), 86–88.

Acts 20:35, while the formula used in Acts recurs in 1 Clement 13:1 and 46:7. Moreover, the description of the apostolic succession in 1 Clement 42:3–4 seems to contain echoes of various passages from Luke–Acts and the Pauline epistles.[1] In my opinion Clement definitely knew the book.

One more book known to Clement deserves mention. This is the 'scripture' which he quotes against the 'double-minded' (23:3–4), probably a Jewish apocryphal document.[2] A slightly different, and longer, version of the same quotation occurs in 2 Clement 11:2–4, where it is ascribed to 'the prophetic discourse'.

It is quite evident that for Clement, a Christian deeply influenced by Jewish ways of thinking even though he often expresses his thought in ways related to Greek rhetoric and even popular philosophy, the primary written authority is the Greek Old Testament, along with some Jewish apocryphal writings from which he derives a saying of Moses (17:6), the 'scripture' about double-mindedness (23:3–4), and such a saying as 'Cling to the saints' (46:2). He certainly knows the book of Judith and uses it, along with Esther, to provide an example of 'womanly manliness' (55:3–6). He seems to quote from an apocryphal version of Ezekiel, but this may be known to him through the anthology which we have suggested he used.

He never refers to New Testament writings as scripture, and the one instance in which he employs the word 'gospel' (47:2) reflects Philippians 3:15, where—as in Clement's own sentence—the word means 'proclamation'. On the other hand, the deeds (especially the sacrifice) of Jesus and his words are exceedingly important to Clement, and he speaks

---

1 Luke 1:1; Acts 1:3, 2:4; Luke 19:11; Acts 14:23; 1 Cor. 16:15; Phil. 1:1.

2 E. Nestle in *Zeitschrift für die neutestamentliche Wissenschaft* 1 (1900), 180.

three times of remembering the words of Christ or of the Lord Jesus. In two of the three instances it seems likely that he has written records in mind, as is the case (though less certainly) in the third instance. If he knew Acts, he probably knew Luke.

When he speaks of 'the epistle' of Paul to the Corinthians (47:1) he certainly does not mean that Paul wrote only one epistle; his allusions to other epistles conclusively prove that he knew a larger collection, although we cannot be sure that it included 2 Corinthians. Along with it, though perhaps not as part of the collection, went the Epistle to the Hebrews. There are no convincing traces of the Pastoral Epistles; perhaps at this time they were in circulation only in Asia Minor and possibly in Crete, the areas to which they were addressed.

These books, gospels, Acts, and epistles alike, possessed authoritative meaning because they recorded the teaching and the deeds of Christ and the apostles. They were not regarded as 'scripture', however, and in Clement's time and geographical setting (Rome and also Corinth) there was no notion of a New Testament canon comparable to that of the Old Testament.

The other book ascribed to Clement is essentially a sermon delivered in a Christian assembly at some unknown time. If we allow for the difference between an official letter and a sermon it becomes possible, but by no means certain, that the two documents were written by the same person. The general outlook of 2 Clement is not remarkably different from that of 1 Clement, and it would appear that both reflect the Hellenistic-Jewish Christianity present at Rome (and, unfortunately for our analysis, probably elsewhere) early in the second century. It is significant that in both documents we find quotations, made independently, from the Jewish apocryphal writing which 1 Clement (23:3) calls 'scripture' and 2 Clement (11:2) calls 'the prophetic word'. Moreover, in 2 Clement as in 1 Clement there are allusions to Romans, 1 Corinthians, Galatians, Ephesians, Philippians, and Hebrews, as well as (perhaps) to James and 1 Peter. In other words, a common 'library' seems to underlie the two works.

Furthermore, the words ascribed to Christ or the Lord or even 'God' (13:4; cf. 1:1) in form resemble the words cited in 1 Clement; they reflect either a combination of Matthew with Luke or a tradition somewhat independent of both gospels. In one instance, however, we read (2:4), after a quotation from Isaiah, that 'another scripture also says, "I come not to call righteous but sinners" '—and this quotation occurs in Matthew 9:13 and Mark 2:17. This passage proves that, unlike the earlier Clement, the author of 2 Clement regards some gospel (perhaps Matthew, usually better known than Mark) as scripture.

We might suppose, then, that 2 Clement would reflect the creation of a definite New Testament canon, at least as far as the gospels are concerned. Such does not seem to be the case, however, for our canonical gospels are certainly not the only authorities he uses as sources for the sayings of Jesus. In chapter 4, section 5 he quotes something the Lord said, and while it resembles what we find in Matthew 7:22 and Luke 13:27 it is not very close to either verse. In chapter 5 he goes on to provide a similar quotation, this time presented in dialogue form.

The Lord said, 'You will be like lambs in the midst of wolves.' Peter answered him and said, 'If then the wolves rend the lambs?'	'Behold, I send you forth like lambs in the midst of wolves' (Luke 10:3)

Jesus said to Peter,	('I say to you my friends',
'Let the lambs not fear the	Luke 12:4)
wolves after they [the	
lambs] die;	
and you, fear not those	'Fear not those who kill the
who kill you and cannot do	body and afterwards have
more to you,	nothing more to do . . .
but fear him who, after you	fear him who, after killing
die,	[you],
has power over soul and	has power ('soul and body',
body to cast them into the	Matt. 10:28) to cast into the
gehenna of fire.'	gehenna' (Luke 12:4–5) ('of
	fire', Matt. 5:22, 18:9)

It is obvious that Lucan and Matthean expressions are combined and that, in addition, they are provided with a setting quite similar to the dialogue of Jesus and Peter about lambs in John 21:15–17. Either synoptic traditions or these synoptic gospels have been given dialogue form in a manner reminiscent of the apocryphal *Gospel of Thomas* (see Chapter VII). Unfortunately we cannot tell whether the quotation in 2 Clement comes from oral tradition or from such an apocryphal gospel.

Another statement, in chapter 12, is considerably farther from the synoptic gospels or John. Here we read that 'when the Lord himself was asked by someone when his kingdom would come, he said, "When the two will be one and the outside as the inside and the male with the female neither male nor female" '. Something close to this is found in the *Gospel of Thomas* (p. 85, lines 20–35), and Clement of Alexandria (*Str.* 3, 92, 2) quotes the *Gospel of the Egyptians* to this effect, giving Jesus' reply to a similar question:

When you tread on the garment of shame and when the two become one and the male with the female neither male nor female.

But the author of 2 Clement is certainly not following the *Gospel of the Egyptians*; for him the flesh is no garment of shame but a temple of God (9:3). He must be relying on some other, less 'Gnostic' book, or on oral tradition. But it is obvious that whether book or tradition, the Lord's words conveyed by it are just as authoritative as the saying contained in 'scripture'.

A rather obscurely allegorical passage in chapter 14 enables us to see somewhat more clearly what authorities are important for this author.

> I do not suppose that you are ignorant [a Pauline expression, Rom. 1:13, 11:25, 1 Cor. 10:1, 12:1, 1 Thess. 4:13] that the living 'Church is the body of Christ' (Eph. 5:23). For the scripture says, 'God made man male and female' (Gen. 1:27): the male is Christ, the female is the Church (cf. Eph. 5:32). And furthermore the books and the apostles declare that the Church is not merely present (cf. Gal. 4:25) but was from the beginning (cf. Eph. 3:9–11, 5:31–32). For it was spiritual, like our Jesus, and 'was made manifest in the last days' (1 Pet. 1:20) to save us. The Church, as being spiritual, was made manifest in the flesh of Jesus (cf. Eph. 5:29).

Scripture obviously includes the Old Testament, and some gospel-writings as well (as we have learned from 2:4); but the letters of the apostles (apparently Paul and Peter, at least) are not scripture. It is hard to tell what 'the books and the apostles' means. Conceivably the phrase is used for 'the books of the apostles and the apostles as the authors of books'.

The limits of the canon in 2 Clement are fairly clear. On the one side stands scripture; the Old Testament and some gospel-book. On the other, the Pauline epistles are not scripture. The middle ground is harder to define. Traditions about Jesus have the same authority as his scriptural sayings, but in 2 Clement there is certainly no idea of a New Testament canon.

The principal difference between 1 and 2 Clement, then, lies in the one instance in which 2 Clement refers to a gospel saying as 'scripture'. Such an identification is not to be found in 1 Clement, and it would seem, therefore, that in 2 Clement we are moving toward an idea of New Testament books as scripture like the Old Testament, especially since the sayings of Jesus, at least partly known in written form, can be ascribed to God. The situation remains fluid, however. Presumably the Jewish Christians in the Roman community (if 2 Clement comes from Rome) still believed that the term 'scripture' should be reserved for the Old Testament and the apocryphal literature transmitted along with it.

VI

The witness of the Apostolic Fathers: Hellenistic Christianity

In this chapter, as we have indicated, we intend to discuss the writings of Ignatius, Polycarp, and 'Barnabas'. (1) Ignatius was bishop of Antioch early in the second century, and on his way through Asia Minor to martyrdom at Rome he wrote two kinds of letters: those to correspondents whose acquaintance he had made during his journey, and the one to the Roman church, asking not to be saved from death. These letters were collected by Polycarp of Smyrna after Ignatius' departure. (2) Somewhat later, Polycarp wrote either one or two letters to the church at Philippi. It has been thought that he wrote two because at one point (9:1-2) he speaks as if Ignatius were dead and at another point (13:2) he asks for news about him. It may be that the passages can be reconciled; but even if they cannot, there is no reason to assume that the later letter is *much* later. (3) The Epistle of Barnabas is very hard to date; its use of 2 Esdras and 2 Baruch suggests the early second century, while the rebuilding of the temple after a war (16:4) probably suggests a period between A.D. 130 and 135. The documents in question thus probably extend over a period of twenty to twenty-five years—no more.

Of the three authors involved, Ignatius is unquestionably

the most interesting and, indeed, exciting. The fact that
scholars in the twenties accused him of being an 'obsessed
neurotic' is hardly a point against him at a time when
psychological insight is more widespread. Certainly he had a
'martyr-complex', since he was determined, as a Christian
already condemned to death, to be a martyr. For our purposes
it is almost equally important to observe that he represents
gentile Christianity, deeply influenced by Greek rhetoric,[1]
and moves toward the formation of a New Testament
because of his insistence on the primacy of the gospel.

One of Ignatius' most striking characteristics was that he
identified his life as Christian, bishop, and sacrificial martyr
with the life and work of Jesus and of the apostle Paul. This
fact has the greatest importance for his use, possible and
probable, of various New Testament books. The books he
found most important were the ones in which he found
statements relevant to his conception of himself and of
fellow-Christians.

We begin with the clearest possible testimonies, those in
which he mentions the apostle Paul and the relation of
Christians to him. In Ephesians 11:2 he speaks of the
Ephesian Christians, who 'always agreed with the apostles
in the power of Jesus Christ'. Such agreement is obviously
reflected in Paul's farewell discourse at Miletus with the
presbyter-bishops of the Ephesian church (Acts 20:18–35),
and it is clear from what Ignatius goes on to say (Eph. 12)
that he has Paul in mind. First he imitates the Pauline antitheses; then he explicitly calls the Ephesians 'fellow-initiates
with Paul, the sanctified, the well attested, the one worthy
of blessing—in whose footsteps may I be found when I
attain to God[2]—who in every letter makes mention of you

1 On Ignatius' style see H. Riesenfeld in *Texte und Untersuchungen*
79 (1961), 312–22.
2 1 Peter 2:21 speaks of following in Christ's footsteps of suffering.

in Christ Jesus'. Paul had been given the sanctity, the attestation, and the blessing potentially shared by all Christians (and Ignatius is deeply concerned with sharing in the universal Christian goals, Eph. 11:2, Smyrn. 7:1), but clearly he had already attained to God (cf. the anticipation of this in Phil. 3:13–14) and Christians could be proud of being 'fellow-initiates' (Phil. 4:12) with him. Like Peter, Paul was an apostle; he was free (1 Cor. 9:1) as a freedman of Christ (1 Cor. 7:22), as Ignatius says (Rom. 4:3). Ignatius is like him; just as for Paul the world has been crucified through Christ (Gal. 6:14), so for Ignatius his 'lust' (*erōs*) has been crucified and he no longer desires the world (Rom. 7:2). Just as Paul no longer lives, but Christ lives in him (Gal. 2:20), so Ignatius has Christ within himself (Rom. 6:3), and as Paul can say, 'Not I but the grace of God' (1 Cor. 15:10), so Ignatius can say, 'Not I but the love of Jesus Christ' (Trall. 6:1) or 'not I but Jesus Christ' (Philad. 5:1).

This does not mean that Ignatius regards himself as an apostle. As for Clement of Rome, for him the apostles belong to a past historical period. They were subject to Christ and to the Father (Magn. 13:2; cf. 1 Clem. 42:1–2), and the Lord, united with the Father, acted through them (Magn. 7:1). They constituted a council or a college, analogous to the presbyters of Ignatius' own day (Magn. 6:1; Trall. 2:2, 3:1; Philad. 5:1; Smyrn. 8:1). Like the Lord, they gave decrees, still valid in the Church (Magn. 13:1). At the same time, the parallel presbyters/apostles means that their work still continues, and Ignatius describes the vocation of the bishop of Philadelphia in terms based on Paul's description of his own calling (Philad. 1:1; Gal. 1:1).

This is to say that Ignatius takes very seriously Paul's words in 1 Corinthians 11:1: 'be imitators of me, as I am of Christ'; and in 1 Thessalonians 1:6: 'you became imitators of us and of the Lord, receiving the word in great tribulation with joy in the Holy Spirit'. Thus Ignatius urges the Ephesians to be imitators of the Lord (Eph. 10:3) and immediately proceeds to quote Pauline counsel (1 Cor. 6:7) about suffering voluntarily; he urges the Philadelphians to be imitators of Jesus Christ (Philad. 7:2)—as he was an imitator of his Father (a theme both Pauline and Johannine). And as Paul speaks of imitating God 'as Christ loved us and gave himself for us' (Eph. 5:1–2), so Ignatius can tell of imitating God by giving (Trall. 1:1) and by self-giving (Eph. 1:1; Rom. 6:3).

To be like Paul and like Christ is to offer oneself as a sacrifice. Paul has been granted the gift not only of believing in Christ but also of suffering for him (Phil. 1:29); indeed, he is being 'poured out' as a sacrificial offering for the Philippians' faith (2:17); he hopes to 'gain Christ and be found in him' (3:8–9) and to 'know him and the power of his resurrection and fellowship with his sufferings, conformed to his death, if somehow I may attain to resurrection from the dead' (3:10–11). Paul rejoices in his sufferings on behalf of the Colossians and fills up 'what is lacking in the tribulations of Christ . . . on behalf of his body, the Church' (Col. 1:24).[1]

Ignatius regards his own work as substantially identical with Paul's. He is eager to suffer (Trall. 4:2), indeed to suffer with Jesus Christ (Smyrn. 4:2). By his suffering he will attain to God (Philad. 7:1) and to the resurrection (Rom 4:3). He is dying for God (Rom. 4:1); he desires to 'be poured out' as a libation for God and through dying rise again (Rom. 2:2), and to be found to be a sacrifice (Rom. 4:2).

Like Paul, Ignatius uses the word *peripsēma* of himself (Eph. 8:1, 18:1; 1 Cor. 4:13). This word has sacrificial overtones absent in Paul's letter but fully present in Ignatius' mind; he is a victim on behalf of the Ephesian Christians.

1 See also Eph. 3:1, 13; 2 Tim. 2:10–12, 4:6.

Similarly he can speak of purifying or consecrating himself for his readers (Eph. 8:1; Trall. 13:3; cf. John 17:19), and four times he uses of himself the sacrificial term *antipsychon* (Eph. 21:1; Smyrn. 10:2; Polyc. 2:3, 6:1) also found in the contemporary 4 Maccabees. At one point, indeed, he comes close to identifying his own flesh with the flesh of Jesus as the bread of God (John 6:33, 51), but he draws back and speaks of 'pure bread of Christ' (Rom. 4:1).

These examples clearly demonstrate that Ignatius is a significant example not only of 'Christ-mysticism' but also, and more especially, of 'Paul-mysticism'. He is not Paul, but the spirit of Paul lives in him. But since Ignatius wrote his letters nearly two generations after Paul's death, it is a question—at least hypothetically—how he knew what he did about Paul. Conceivably he could have known about him from oral tradition, either at Antioch or in Asia Minor; but this kind of knowledge would not account for the innumerable echoes of Paul's letters in those of Ignatius. It is much more likely that his mind was saturated with memories of Paul's letters, which he applied to himself. For example, when he greets the Trallians 'in apostolic fashion', his salutation contains clear echoes of Colossians 1:19–20 and 27, partly because the 'spiritual knowledge' of the Trallians seems to have resembled that to which some Colossians laid claim (Trall. 5:2; cf. Col. 1:16, 2:18).

Ignatius even takes isolated passages from 1 Corinthians (especially) and applies them to himself at unexpected points; two examples will suffice.

> I need your love, so that I may be judged worthy of the lot which I am set to obtain, 'lest I be found a castaway' (1 Cor. 9:27; Trall. 12:3).

> I become more of a disciple because of their [his guards'] wrongdoing, 'but not by this am I justified' (1 Cor. 4:4; Rom. 5:1).

In all his church letters except Philadelphians (to a church with which his relations were not altogether cordial) Ignatius makes use of something like a formula—again derived from 1 Corinthians. He refers to the church in Syria, and then continues thus:

> being the least of the faithful there (Eph. 21:2)
>
> whence I am not worthy to be called (Magn. 14)
>
> whence I am not worthy to be counted, being the least of them (Trall. 13:1)
>
> I am ashamed to be counted one of them, for I am not worthy, being the least of them and an abortion; but I have obtained mercy to be someone (Rom. 9:2).
>
> I am not worthy to be from there, being the least of them; but by God's will I have been judged worthy, not by my conscience but by the grace of God (Smyrn. 11:1).

What binds all these passages together is a passage never quoted but obviously present, from 1 Corinthians.

> Last of all he appeared to me as to an abortion. For I am the least of the apostles, unworthy to be called an apostle, because I persecuted the Church of God; but by God's grace I am what I am (1 Cor. 15:8–10).

Virginia Corwin has suggested that the passage is in Ignatius' mind because he felt himself responsible for divisions at Antioch;[1] more probably, in view of Paul's language, Ignatius himself had once persecuted Christians, and perhaps had been responsible for martyrdoms.

However this may be explained, it is a fact that 1 Corinthians is 'written on his heart'; his letters are crowded with allusions to it. And this means that conventional categories

1 *St Ignatius and Christianity at Antioch* (New Haven, 1960), 27–29.

such as 'scripture' or 'canon' are not very relevant. Obviously 1 Corinthians is supremely authoritative for Ignatius, even though he never says he is quoting from it or calls it 'scripture'.

Though for Ignatius 1 Corinthians was the most meaningful of the Pauline epistles, it is quite clear that he was acquainted with a larger collection which apparently included Romans, 1 Corinthians, Galatians, Ephesians, Philippians, Colossians, 1 Thessalonians, and perhaps 2 Thessalonians. It is possible, but not probable, that he knew the Pastoral Epistles; the parallels—rather infrequent—probably reflect similar situations, not use of the letters.

(1) Ignatius takes phrases from Romans. 'Where is boasting?' (Rom. 3:27) is found in a passage based entirely on Pauline expressions (Eph. 18:1). 'Newness of eternal life' (Eph. 19:3) is clearly based on Romans 6:4—which, with the following verse, is imitated in Trallians 9:2. Paul's discussion of flesh and spirit in Romans 8:5–8 is imitated in Ephesians 8:2, and his mention of suffering 'with Christ' (Rom. 8:17) recurs in Smyrnaeans 4:2.

(2) The Philadelphian bishop, like the apostle Paul (Gal. 1:1), obtained his ministry not from himself or 'through men' (Philad. 1:1). Ignatius' contrast of Judaism with the grace of God (Magn. 8:1) seems to be based on Galatians 5:2–4. Elsewhere we find several phrases from Galatians which Ignatius uses in his own way. Paul said that if the Judaizers were right, Christ died in vain (Gal. 2:21); Ignatius says that if the Docetists are right he himself is dying in vain (Trall. 10; in a context based on 1 Corinthians). The phrase 'the scandal of the cross' (Eph. 18:1) comes from Galatians 5:11—again, used in a context of Pauline expressions. Finally, when Ignatius says that his *erōs* has been crucified (Rom. 7:2) he is imitating Paul's expression, 'For me the world has been crucified' (Gal. 6:14).

(3) From Ephesians Ignatius derives not only the passages we have already discussed but also some of his expressions about the unity of the Church; he imitates Ephesians 4:3–6 in Magnesians 7:1 and Philadelphians 4, and speaks of unity in Polycarp 1:2, using a phrase from Ephesians 4:2. Men are 'to love their wives as the Lord loved the Church' (Polyc. 5:1; Eph. 5:25–29). Similarly, the phrase 'in one body of his Church' (Smyrn. 1:2) is based on Ephesians 2:16 (perhaps with Col. 1:18). The Lord's 'dwelling in' us, reflected in love (Eph. 15:3) is an idea derived from Ephesians 3:17–19; the phrase 'children of light', associated with truth (Philad. 2:1) comes from Ephesians 5:8–9. In Magnesians 13:2 Ignatius asks for subjection to 'the bishop and to one another, as Jesus Christ was subject to the Father and the apostles were to Christ and the Father'; subjection to one another comes from Ephesians 5:21, and the Church's subjection to Christ from Ephesians 5:24. Finally, the picture of the Christians' putting on the armor of God (Polyc. 6:2) comes either from Ephesians 6:11–17 or from 1 Thessalonians 5:8.

(4) In addition to the Philippians passages discussed above, Ignatius seems to make use of such language at two points in Smyrnaeans: the ideas of thinking and of perfection (11:3) are also related in Philippians 3:15, and the ability to do everything necessary because of the power of Christ (4:2) is based on Philippians 4:13. Philippians 4:12 may also be echoed in Ignatius' description of the Ephesians as 'fellow-initiates with Paul' (Eph. 12:2).

(5) Colossians, as we have seen, is echoed in Ignatius' Trallians at the beginning. There are other allusions as well. In Trallians 5:2 he states that he can understand 'heavenly things' (*ta epourania*), and in Smyrnaeans 6:1 he says that 'heavenly things', including rulers visible and invisible, will be condemned if they do not believe in the blood of Christ.

('Things visible and invisible' are mentioned in Romans 5:3.) Here he probably has Colossians 1:16–20 in mind, for in those verses Paul mentions heavenly and earthly powers, visible and invisible, and speaks of their reconciliation through the blood of the cross. The phrase 'steadfast in faith' (Eph. 10:2) occurs in Colossians 1:23. Finally, the notion that deacons are Ignatius' fellow-slaves (Eph. 2:1; Magn. 2:1; Philad. 4; Smyrn. 12:2) is based on Paul's remark that Epaphras is a fellow-slave and a 'deacon of Christ' for the Colossians (1:7).

(6) As might perhaps be expected, there are few allusions to the Thessalonian letters. The idea of pleasing not men but God, however (Rom. 2:1), seems to come from 1 Thessalonians 2:4, and the injunction to 'pray unceasingly' (Eph. 10:1) is repeated exactly from 1 Thessalonians 5:17. A mention of 'the endurance of Jesus Christ' (Rom. 10:3) may be based on 2 Thessalonians 3:5, but Ignatius also seems to reflect something like Matthew 10:22 (24:13) when he speaks of enduring to the end.

As we have said, the possible allusions to the Pastoral Epistles probably reflect a common viewpoint in relation to heresy. It may be, however, that 2 Timothy 1:16 is reflected in Smyrnaeans 10:2 and that 2 Timothy 2:4 is paraphrased in Polycarp 6:2. Perhaps this letter, or the Pastorals as a group, were in limited circulation in the area around Ephesus.

There is one more letter with which Ignatius seems to be acquainted. This is 1 Peter, clearly sent from Rome to a wide area which included Asia Minor (1:1). It seems likely that Ignatius refers to this letter (as well as, perhaps, 1 Clement) when he says that the Roman church has taught others and asks that their instructions may stand fast (Rom. 3:1). The instructions must be those to rejoice as one takes part in the sufferings of Christ and to suffer as a genuine Christian (1 Pet. 4:12–16)—for this is what Ignatius discusses in the third chapter of Romans. His short quotation from Proverbs 3:34 in Ephesians 5:3 does not prove that he was using 1 Pet. 5:5 (or James 4:6), for he knew the book of Proverbs and his word order is not that of Peter or James.

The collection of letters which Ignatius knew, then, and knew practically by heart, contained the following letters (listed in order of frequency of use): 1 Corinthians, Ephesians, Romans, Galatians, Philippians, Colossians, 1 (-2?) Thessalonians, and 1 Peter. This frequency of usage indicates nothing about the way in which the letters were collected or transmitted, for Ignatius' use of them depends largely on the circumstances in relation to which he was writing his own letters. It is no accident that the ones he uses most often (1 Corinthians, Ephesians) are those in which the unity of the Church—practical and theoretical— is most strongly emphasized. He does not call these letters 'scripture', however, and we have no reason to suppose that he regarded them as such.

Indeed, in his letters only two quotations, both from the book of Proverbs, are introduced by the formula 'it is written' (Eph. 5:3, perhaps based on 1 Pet. 5:5; Magn. 12). The same formula also occurs in Ignatius' account (Philad. 8:2) of a debate he had, apparently with Judaizing Christians at Philadephia. They said to him, 'If I do not find it in the "charters" (*archeia*), I do not believe it in the gospel.' He replied, 'But it is written.' They answered, 'That is just the question.' His response to their hesitation was to affirm that for him 'the "charters" are Jesus Christ, the inviolable sacred "charters" are his cross and death and resurrection, and faith through him'. This account seems to make sense if we assume that the Judaizers wanted proof from the Old Testament 'charters' for some point related to the death and resurrection of Christ, and that Ignatius said that such proof was written there. They then expressed their doubts

D

that it could be found, and he replied by arguing that the foundation of Christian faith is not the Old Testament but Jesus Christ. As he elsewhere says in similar circumstances (Magn. 10:3), 'Christianity did not express its faith as based on Judaism'.

His use of 'it is written' in these passages clearly suggests that like the Judaizers he regarded the Old Testament as 'scripture', the written authority of the Church, and also that neither he nor they knew written gospels which could be regarded as 'scripture'.

This point does not imply, however, that Ignatius did not know written gospels, and we must investigate this question without regard for the question of canonicity or 'scriptural' quality.

On the question of Ignatius' acquaintance with the gospels, the most important recent works are those by C. Maurer (*Ignatius von Antiochien und das Johannesevangelium*, 1949) and H. Koester (*Synoptische Überlieferungen bei den Apostolischen Vätern*, 1957). Maurer endeavors to prove that Ignatius knew the Gospel of John by showing that (1) the way in which John was quoted by other second-century writers is close to the way in which Ignatius seems to quote John, (2) Ignatius' quotations from other documents are as allusive as his presumed quotations from John, and (3) several passages in Ignatius are very close to John. These arguments seem conclusive, although perhaps Ignatius knew the author or the editor of the Fourth Gospel instead of, or in addition to, his book.

The most important parallels are as follows. (1) Ignatius speaks of the Eucharist as 'the bread of God' (Eph. 5:1; Rom. 7:3) and identifies the bread with the flesh of Jesus Christ (cf. Smyrn. 7:1), the wine with his blood (Rom. 7:3). The bread of God is mentioned in John 6:33 and identified with the flesh of Jesus in John 6:51–58, where we also find drinking his blood discussed. (2) Ignatius speaks of the Spirit, 'which is from God' and 'knows whence it comes and whither it goes' (Philad. 7:1). So in John 8:14 Jesus knows whence he comes and whither he goes, but his opponents do not know this, and in John 3:8 Nicodemus does not know whence the Spirit comes and whither it goes; and men reborn through the Spirit (John 3:5–7) are men generated by God (1:13). (3) According to Philadelphians 9:1 Jesus is 'the door of the Father', as he is the door for the sheep (presumably coming to the Father, John 14:6) in John 10: 7–9. (4) Jesus came forth from the one Father and is with him and departed to him (Magn. 7:2); this teaching is emphasized in John 8:42 (13:3; 14:12, 18; 16:10, 17, 18). (5) The idea that Jesus 'raised himself' (Smyrn. 2) is expressed in John 10:18 (5:26.)[1]

The absence of exact quotations is no more striking than the absence of exact quotations from 1 Corinthians.

As for the synoptic parallels, we must insist upon certain methodological criteria before we discuss any of them. (1) We have already seen that Ignatius uses the Pauline epistles, which he certainly knew in written form, in a very free manner. (2) We have argued that he knew either the Gospel of John or Johannine ideas and used it or them in the same way. (3) These points imply that if he knew any synoptic gospels he presumably exercised considerable freedom in in quoting from them. On the other hand, (4) since we do not definitely know that he knew any synoptic gospels we cannot usually be sure whether he is alluding to books or to oral traditions.

Beyond these points lies the basic question of the use of memory, to which we shall return (Chapter VII). When an author alludes to something which we know is written in a

1 Other theological parallels in *Ermeneutica e tradizione* (ed. E. Castelli, Rome, 1963), 191–92.

book, it is not usually possible to determine whether or not he derived it from the book. The words to which he alludes may have come to him from the book or from someone else's quotation from or allusion to the book, or from a source (oral or written) quite independent of the book. This complicated but authentic picture suggests that dogmatic conclusions, one way or another, are untenable.

Let us begin with two passages in which Ignatius speaks of the baptism of Jesus. (1) In Ephesians 18:2 he says that Jesus was baptized 'so that by the Passion he might purify the water'. For the moment we need not consider either what Ignatius meant or what sources outside the gospels he may have had; it is enough to say that he did not derive this statement from what we find in the synoptic gospels. (2) On the other hand, in a semi-credal passage (Smyrn. 1:1) he states that Jesus was baptized by John 'so that all righteousness might be fulfilled by him'. These words must be related to Matthew 3:15: 'it is fitting for us to fulfill all righteousness'; the words 'fulfill' and 'righteousness' are especially characteristic of Matthew's thought and vocabulary. According to Koester, however, Ignatius relied not on Matthew but on a kerygmatic formula composed by someone else. It is impossible to tell whether or not Koester is right. Could not Ignatius himself compose kerygmatic formulas?

Two passages in his letter to Polycarp (2:1–2) are very close to synoptic parallels.

If you love good disciples it is no credit to you.	If you love those who love you what credit is it to you (Luke 6:32)?
Become wise (sing.) as a serpent—in everything— and guileless—forever— as the dove.	Then become wise (pl.) as the serpents and guileless as the doves (Matt. 10:16).

Certainly Ignatius regards these words as containing proverbial wisdom; he inserts between them two Hellenistic proverbs based on medical practice. But this fact does not imply that he is not relying on his memory of what he has read, at various times, in the Gospels of Luke and Matthew. When Koester says that 'it is more probable that both logia come from the free tradition than that one is derived from Matt., the other from Luke', we can only reply that this conclusion is possible but not probable.

In our opinion Ignatius used whatever written sources he had in a way strikingly similar to that in which the evangelist John used sayings of Jesus[1] and the Old Testament[2]— without any attempt at verbal exactness. He relied on his memory and did not check his references. As E. Flesseman -van Leer has written, 'Ignatius attaches little importance to the authority of scripture as such (though he nowhere denies this importance)'.[3] Indeed, one can go a bit farther than this.

We recall once more that for Ignatius the primary authority is the apostolic preaching about the life, death, and resurrection of Jesus Christ. For him it makes little difference, or none, whether the doctrine has been transmitted in oral or written form. Because the matter is so unimportant it is sometimes hard for us to decide what kind of sources he is using when he tells us about Jesus. The best example of the difficulty is provided in Smyrnaeans 3:1–3.

I know and believe that even after the resurrection he was in the flesh. And when he came to those with Peter he said, 'Take, handle me and see that I am not a bodiless demon.' And immediately they touched him and believed, being mingled

1 T. F. Glasson in *Expository Times* 57 (1946), 111–12.
2 C. Goodwin in *Journal of Biblical Literature* 73 (1954), 61–75.
3 *Tradition and Scripture in the Early Church* (Assen, Holland, 1954), 35.

with his flesh and spirit. Therefore they despised death and were found to be above death. After the resurrection he ate and drank with them as a being of flesh, though spiritually he was united with the Father.

Where do these 'words of Jesus' come from? According to Origen, they came from a *Teaching of Peter*—though this may be just a guess based on the mention of Peter's name. Jerome says they came from the *Gospel of the Hebrews*. Eusebius sagely confesses his ignorance. Conceivably Ignatius is simply paraphrasing Luke 24:39 ('handle me and see, for a spirit does not have flesh and bones . . .')— especially since eating and drinking with the risen Lord is mentioned in this chapter of Luke, as well as in a speech by Peter in Acts 10:41. On the other hand, it is interesting and perhaps significant that in a document close in time, if not in place, to Ignatius we have already found materials related to Peter and the Gospel of Luke but not found in our gospels (2 Clement 5:2–4).

There is no reason to suppose that Ignatius, even though he knew some gospels later regarded as canonical, was restricted to using them only.

Our conclusion is that Ignatius certainly knew a collection of Pauline epistles (at least eight in number) and probably knew two or three gospels (Matthew, John, probably Luke). He did not regard any of the Christian writings as 'scripture', but for him no written document possessed the authority of the gospel about Jesus Christ.

Polycarp of Smyrna

Polycarp certainly knows a collection of Pauline epistles, and he knows that the Philippians also possess a collection, apparently identical with his own. 'When Paul was among you in the presence of the men of that time, he accurately and steadfastly taught the word of truth, and when he was absent he wrote you letters; by studying them you will be able to build yourselves up into the faith given you' (3:2). Polycarp's 'word of truth' looks like an allusion to 2 Timothy (2:15, 18), and after this sentence he goes on to allude to Galatians 4:26 and Romans 13:8—presumably found in the collection he has in mind. Elsewhere (11:3) he refers explicitly to the Philippians as those 'among whom the blessed Paul labored, who are at the beginning of his letter; concerning you he boasts in all the churches which then alone had known the Lord'. Here he seems to be referring to Philippians 4:15 ('the beginning of the gospel') and alluding to 2 Thessalonians 1:4 ('we ourselves boast of you in the churches of God'). Like Clement and Ignatius, Polycarp likes to refer to the particular Pauline epistle which he believes his correspondents value most highly. Thus the words with which he begins his letter, 'I rejoiced greatly with you in the Lord', are borrowed from Philippians 4:10 (2:17), and his mention of their firmly rooted faith (1:2) is probably another echo of Philippians 4:15–17. Similarly the statement that the martyrs 'have not run in vain' (9:2) is based on Paul's words about himself in Philippians 2:16. Finally, Polycarp's injunction to pray for 'the enemies of the cross' (12:3) reflects the phrase of Philippians 3:18.

The Pauline epistles to which Polycarp certainly alludes are Romans, 1 Corinthians, Galatians, Ephesians, Philippians, 2 Thessalonians, 1 Timothy and 2 Timothy. E. Schweizer has suggested that 2 Thessalonians was actually addressed to the Philippians, chiefly because of the allusion mentioned above,[1] but as W. R. Schoedel points out, Polycarp refers to only one letter addressed to them. H. von

1 *Theologische Zeitschrift* 1 (1945), 90–91.

Campenhausen has offered the bold hypothesis that Polycarp himself wrote the Pastoral Epistles,[1] but Polycarp insists on the inferiority of himself to Paul and on the difference between the apostolic age and his own time (3:2); this insistence seems to exclude the possibility that he wrote letters in Paul's name.

In addition, he may know Colossians and almost certainly knows Hebrews. He calls Christ 'the eternal high priest' (12:2; Heb. 6:20, 7:3) and seems to allude to Hebrews 12:28 (6:3). 1 John 4:2–3 or 2 John 7 is also reflected (7:1). Most significantly, he knows 1 Peter and 1 Clement practically by heart; allusions to these letters—which he never mentions or quotes—occur everywhere in his own writing.

The primary authorities to which he refers are 'the Lord himself', 'the apostles, who brought us the gospel', and 'the prophets, who foretold the coming of our Lord' (6:3). In citing the Lord's teaching (2:3) he uses the formula already found in Acts and 1 Clement when he speaks of 'remembering what the Lord taught when he said . . .'; the teaching, as in 1 Clement, is paralleled in Matthew and Luke. Elsewhere (4:1) he refers to 'the commandment of the Lord' and once (7:2) quotes Matthew 26:41 as 'the Lord said'. He has a collection, oral or written, of Jesus' sayings; the exact quotation of Matthew 13:14–15 (6:2) suggests that it was written.

Both the epistles and the sayings are included among the authorities to which he refers when he uses the formula 'knowing that . . .'.

1:3 'by grace you are saved, not by works' (Eph. 2:5–9)
4:1 'we brought nothing into the world and can take nothing out'. (1 Tim. 6:7, just after an apparent allusion to 1 Tim. 6:10)

1 *Sitzungsberichte der Heidelberger Akademie der Wissenschaften* (Philos.-hist. Kl.), 1951, no. 2.

4:3 . . . 'nothing escapes him [God] of reasonings or thoughts'
(1 Clem. 21:3)

5:1 'God is not mocked' (Gal. 6:7)

6:1 'we all owe the debt of sin' (the thought continues with
apparent allusions to Matt. 6:12, Luke 11:4, or Matt. 13:
14–15)

In addition, we should mention 'being persuaded that'
(9:2, with Phil. 2:16) and 'do we not know?' (11:2, with 1
Cor. 6:2). To go still further, we could include arguments
introduced with 'for' like those in 5:3 (1 Pet. 2:11 and 1 Cor.
6:9–10) and 6:2 (Rom. 14:10–12).

It is clear enough that Polycarp regards the statements to
which he refers as authoritative. Did he regard them as
contained in 'scripture'? Certainly he knows of scriptures,
for he tells the Philippians (quoting their letter to him?)
that they are well versed in them, though he himself is not
(12:1).[1] And he goes on to remark, 'as it is said in these
scriptures, "Be angry and sin not", and "Let not the sun
go down upon your wrath."' The first quotation comes from
Psalm 4:5; both occur together in Ephesians 4:26—a letter
which Polycarp knew. Koester[2] and others have supposed
that Polycarp thinks he is quoting from the Old Testament
but, since he is relying on his memory, uses Ephesians
instead. This view may be correct. Although there is nothing
in Ephesians to suggest to the reader that Paul himself is
using the Old Testament, Polycarp has just said that he
does not know the Old Testament well.

Our conclusion is that while Polycarp certainly had a
collection of epistles (at least eight Pauline letters, including
two of the Pastorals; 1 Peter; 1 Clement; 1 or 2 John;

1 Old Testament allusions, in fact, are unusual in his letter: Is.
52:5 (10:3), Jer. 5:4 (11:2), Tobit 4:10, 12:9 (10:2); perhaps Prov. 3:4
(6:1).

2 *Op. cit.*, 113.

Hebrews; the letters of Ignatius) and at least one gospel (Matthew), he did not regard the books as 'scripture'. From this letter it cannot be shown that he knew the Gospel of John, although—given the tradition about his learning from John, the Lord's disciple[1]—we may suspect that he did.

Polycarp's evidence is important not only because he is the first Apostolic Father to provide clear reflections of the Pastoral Epistles but also because he shows that the New Testament books were not definitely regarded as scripture by him any more than by Clement or Ignatius. The Philippians were evidently more concerned with 'scriptures' than he was. The question of 'scripture' was not as important as the question of 'the word of truth' set forth either orally or in writing. At the same time, Polycarp clearly differentiates the apostolic age from his own time and, presumably for this reason, does not use the letters of Ignatius as authorities —even though they 'contain faith, endurance, and all the edification which pertains to our Lord' (13:2).

The Epistle of Barnabas

The use of New Testament writings in the Epistle of Barnabas is especially interesting because of the context in which it occurs. For Barnabas, apparently arguing with Christians tempted by Judaism, the primary authorities are Old Testament writers, chiefly the prophets; he often refers to their writings as 'scripture'. But his Old Testament canon is apparently a very broad one, especially in relation to Jewish apocalyptic writings. He uses 1 Enoch for a prediction of the last times and explicitly refers to Enoch himself as the author (4:3); indeed, he refers to 1 Enoch as

1 Irenaeus in Eusebius, *H. E.* 5, 20, 5.

'scripture' and quotes a verse with the formula 'it is written' (16:5-6). Among the prophets he includes the authors of 2 Esdras (cited, 12:1) and 2 Baruch (cited, 11:9), both of whom wrote during the Christian era. Finally, according to a late manuscript of his work his quotation from one of the Psalms is combined with something from an *Apocalypse of Adam*.

Under these circumstances, the use of 'it is written' to introduce what looks like a quotation from Matthew (20:16 or 22:14), 'Many are called but few are chosen' (4:14), is neither surprising nor significant. To find that the Gospel of Matthew is as 'scriptural' as 1 Enoch does not give Matthew much credit.

At the same time, Barnabas clearly knows Matthew and derives details about the passion of Jesus from it (7:3, 5, 9). Probably he gets from it his reference to Jesus as having come 'not to call the righteous but sinners' (Matt. 9:13, and parallels; Barn. 5:9). He probably also knows the Gospel of John, for after discussing the serpent of Numbers he refers to the 'glory' of Jesus (12:7; cf. John 3:14), and he speaks of Jesus as having been 'pierced' on the cross (John 19:34; Barn. 7:9). Neither Johannine reference is conclusive, however. It may be that Barnabas also knew the Pastoral Epistles. His reference to Jesus as calling sinners, including the apostles, 'lawless beyond all sin' (5:9), reminds us of 1 Timothy 3:15: 'The saying is trustworthy and worthy of full acceptance, that Christ Jesus came into the world to save sinners—of whom I am the chief.' And his mention of 'grace', 'manifested', and 'the destruction of death' (5:6) recalls a similar combination of words in 2 Timothy 1:9-10.

None of these passages, however, probable or improbable as allusions, suggests in any way that Barnabas regarded the New Testament documents as 'scripture' in a sense more significant than that in which he regarded the Jewish apocalyptic writings. He is no witness to the development of a New Testament canon.

Our examination of these writings of the more Hellenistic among the Apostolic Fathers clearly indicates that the use of New Testament books was more common among them than among Jewish Christians. In this regard, both 1 Clement and 2 Clement belong to the 'Hellenistic wing'. For all alike the Old Testament, either with or without Jewish apocalyptic literature, was regarded as 'scripture' and the New Testament writings were not so regarded. This is not to say that the New Testament writings lacked authority. It is simply to say that the question of 'scripture' was not especially significant. When the author of 2 Clement apparently quoted Matthew as 'scripture', and when Polycarp apparently quoted Ephesians in the same way, their citations are not much more important than the one found in Barnabas. We cannot say that a New Testament canon had come into existence as yet. We can say that among gentile Christians the way toward a New Testament was being prepared.

VII

The problem of the New Testament Apocrypha

In addition to the books later regarded as canonical, there were quite a few other documents in circulation among Christians early in the second century and possibly earlier. Clearly there was precedent for the use of such documents in communities like the one at Qumran, where such an apocalyptic book as 1 Enoch was read with enthusiasm. The Epistle of Jude reveals the existence of an analogous situation among some Christians, for in it we find a clear allusion to the apocryphal Assumption of Moses (Jude 9) and an explicit quotation from 1 Enoch (Jude 14–15). Early Christian reading was not confined to the Old Testament. Moreover, the fact that early Christians continued to produce their own literature—e.g. the book of Revelation 'toward the end of the reign of Domitian'—did not at first encourage the idea of a fixed collection of New Testament books. Adherents of various minority groups within, and on the edge of, the churches were not content to provide exegesis of the books generally accepted but proceeded to create additional gospels, acts, epistles, apocalypses, etc.

Their activities may have been encouraged by statements like the ones we find in John 20:30 and 21:25: 'Jesus performed many other signs in the presence of his disciples which are not written in this book', and 'there are many other things which Jesus did; if they were individually recorded, I think that the world itself could not contain the books that could be written'. Gnostics and others may have proceeded to test this hypothesis.

Unfortunately we have practically no means of telling when the movement toward writing the 'extra-canonical' literature began. In our opinion none of the 'canonical' gospels was written much later than A.D. 75, even though oral traditions about Jesus' life and teaching continued to circulate for a considerable period of time thereafter. If we look at the writings of the Apostolic Fathers (Chapters IV–VI) we see that there are several passages which resemble what we find, or can reasonably suppose to have been, in apocryphal gospels (e.g., 2 Clem. 12:2; Ignatius; Smyrn. 3:2), but we do not know that these passages came from written documents rather than from oral traditions. We can certainly say that the materials used in the apocryphal gospels were in existence; we cannot say that the gospels themselves had been written. Eusebius tells us that a story related by Papias was also to be found in the apocryphal *Gospel of the Hebrews*, but this statement does not prove that Papias used this gospel. On the other hand, the fact that we do not know that apocryphal documents were in existence does not indicate that they did not exist. They may have arisen as early as the end of the first century. Indeed, if we take literally what Luke says about his 'many' predecessors who had undertaken to compile accounts of Christian origins (Luke 1:1–2), the 'many' may have included writers whose works were later rejected.

In earlier eras of historical study, there was widespread acceptance of the view that in all early Christian literature one could trace 'development' and that one could then use this 'development' for dating documents. Even if such development could be shown to have existed in every area of Christian life and thought—and this has not been shown —it could hardly provide an accurate means of dating. And when we deal with apocryphal documents which reflect the views of little groups within the Church, our knowledge of the history of these groups is so limited that we are unable to correlate the documents with it.

In recent times it is often suggested that many of the apocryphal books come from about A.D. 140. The grounds for this opinion are not altogether clear. We know that Marcion presented his one gospel (a version of Luke) to the Roman church about this time, but this fact tells us nothing about the existence or the nature of other gospels.

It is rather difficult to say what the authority of some of these apocryphal writings was in the course of the second century, because we possess so little Christian literature from the period. We have to look for traces of usage or non-usage and combine these with attitudes which often come from a later time. For example, we know of a gospel, a 'kerygma', and an apocalypse ascribed to Peter. Possible traces of the gospel occur in the *Dialogue* by Justin (about 160), but it really comes on the scene only when it is being rejected by Serapion of Antioch (about 190). The *Kerygma* was used by the Valentinian Gnostic Heracleon and by Clement of Alexandria without any hesitation; Origen, on the other hand, was most uncertain about its authority.[1] We find the apocalypse in Clement's writings, but only in his *Eclogae propheticae*.[2] Again, the gospels *According to the Hebrews* and *According to the Egyptians* occur in Clement's writings up to the point at which he says there are only four gospels (see Chapter XI); Origen uses *Hebrews* three

1 Clement, *Str.* 1, 182, 3; 2, 68, 2; 6, 39, 2–43, 3; 6, 48, 1–2; 6, 58, 1; 6, 128, 1–3; *Eclog. proph.* 58; Heracleon in Origen, *Ioh. comm.* 13, 17.
2 *Eclog. proph.* 41, 2; 48, 1; 49, 1.

times, but expresses doubts about its authority on each occasion, and he explicitly rejects *Egyptians*.[1] Hippolytus (early third century) says that the Naassene Gnostics use the *Gospel of Thomas*; Origen rejects it absolutely.[2]

From these facts one can probably draw the following conclusions. (1) Various apocryphal gospels and other writings were apparently used in various localities such as Alexandria and Antioch without much hesitation during the second century. It is even possible that the *Gospel according to the Egyptians* was used at Rome, since parallels to it occur in 2 Clement. (2) Toward the end of the century non-Gnostic writers came to be much more cautious in employing these writings. Irenaeus, Clement, and Origen concur in stating that the Church as a whole accepts four, and only four, gospels.[3] (3) Nevertheless, one must not suppose that logic was rigorously employed in this connection. Clement stopped quoting explicitly from *Hebrews* after stating that there were four gospels; instead, he quoted from the book without naming his source (*Str.* 5, 96, 3). Origen expressed his doubts about this gospel but quoted from it just the same and provided exegesis of it. (4) This means that while in theory there were four gospels, in practise—perhaps even more among Christians who did *not* write books—there were more. After all, though Serapion of Antioch finally banned the *Gospel of Peter*, at first he was perfectly willing for it to be read (see Chapter X). In view of the fact that the situation would have been much clearer if only four gospels were being used, we must suppose that popular pressure was responsible for the semi-acceptance of other books. And if such popular pressure existed, it was

1 *Jer. hom.* 15, 4; *Ioh. comm.* 2, 12; *Matt. comm.* 15, 14; Egyptians: *Luc. hom.* 1.

2 Hippolytus, *Ref.* 5, 7, 20; Origen, *Luc. hom.* 1.

3 Irenaeus, *Adv. haer.* 3, 11, 11; Clement, *Str.* 3, 93, 1; Origen, *Luc. hom.* 1.

probably due to the weight of previous custom. We conclude, then, that before the end of the second century many Christians used more than four gospels, even though the 'canonical' four were the ones most widely employed. We should add that some Christians relied upon only one gospel—either one of the four or one more highly favored by a particular sect.

The most significant of the extant apocryphal gospels is the *Gospel of Thomas*, parts of which were found in Greek sixty years ago (but not identified). The whole gospel was discovered at Nag Hammadi in Eygpt about 1945, in a Coptic version of the fourth century. It consists of about 115 sayings, parables, and brief dialogues ascribed to Jesus; it begins with the statement that 'these are the secret words which Jesus spoke while alive and Didymus Thomas wrote down'. R. North has classified their contents in relation to the synoptic tradition as follows: (1) synoptic sayings reproduced identically (about 25); (2) synoptic sayings expressed more succinctly; (3) synoptic sayings slightly amplified or combined; (4) synoptic sayings altered, usually in a Gnostic direction. In addition, there are sayings which have no New Testament parallels—a few rather like the 'canonical' sayings, more of them Gnostic in tone.[1] The question has arisen whether the author of *Thomas* was relying on the written synoptic gospels or on oral traditions of various kinds. In my own view, *Thomas* is based, at least in large measure, on the written gospels of Matthew and Luke,[2] but it remains possible that its author used not only these gospels but oral traditions as well.

The way in which he arranged his materials is rather mysterious. Quite a few of the sayings are put together in

1 *Catholic Biblical Quarterly* 24 (1962), 164–65.
2 See R. M. Grant–D. N. Freedman–W. R. Schoedel, *The Secret Sayings of Jesus* (New York–London, 1960).

relation to common subject matter; others seem to be cor-related only by verbal association and thus *perhaps* reflect oral transmission (see Chapter IV). S. Giversen[1] has pointed out a peculiarity in the book as it now stands, and as it stood in the Greek fragments: the question about fasting, prayer, almsgiving, and food laws which the disciples ask in saying 6 is not answered until saying 14, and sayings 7–13 are not related to the subject. Does this suggest that the author intentionally disarranged his materials so that only the Gnostic reader could understand them? Or that a later editor—not too late, since the present arrangement is reflected in the Greek fragments from about A.D. 200—is responsible for the situation?

Similar difficulties arise in regard to the so-called *Gospel of Philip*, discovered in the same volume of Gnostic docu-ments. This 'gospel' is much less a gospel than is *Thomas*, and there are very few sayings of Jesus in it, or references to his actions. Instead, there is considerable exegesis of what seem to be New Testament books, including Matthew, Luke, and John, some of the Pauline epistles (Romans, 1–2 Corinthians, Galatians, Philippians, and perhaps Ephesians and Hebrews), and finally 1 Peter and 1 John.[2] These books are all, with the possible exception of Hebrews, attested by Valentinian Gnostics, from whose circles *Philip* almost certainly comes (see Chapter VIII). At this point we are primarily concerned, however, not with *Philip*'s sources or canon but with his arrangement of his materials. To trace any sequence in it, as a whole, is practically impossible. His work seems to reflect the intention of purposely confusing the uninitiate reader.

The question of arrangement is fairly important because

1 *Acta Orientalia* 25 (1961), 332–38.
2 Cf. R. McL. Wilson, *The Gospel of Philip* (London–New York, 1962), 7.

the gospels accepted by the churches were at least relatively clearly arranged. The reader has some confidence that he knows what is being discussed. A consecutive and rather consistent story is being told. In an apocryphal gospel like *Thomas* (leaving *Philip* out of account, since it is so different) the reader can tell what is being discussed only within limited sections of the book. Only a perceptive eye like Giversen's would note that separate sayings should really be read together.

Some apocryphal gospels, however, seem to have been more like those generally accepted by Christians. Among these were the gospels *According to the Hebrews* and *According to the Egyptians* which we have already mentioned. And while we really know nothing about the ways in which their authors arranged their materials, the fragments from these gospels which we possess suggest that they were closer to the synoptics, at least, in form, than to the *Gospel of Thomas*.

Further information about the way in which gospels were created in the early second century is provided by the 'fragments of an unknown gospel' published by H. I. Bell and T. C. Skeat in 1935. Two of the fragments are medium-sized (roughly 12 × 9 cm) while the third is tiny (6 × 2.3 cm). The handwriting points toward the first half of the second century. Here we reproduce in English what can be made out with some measure of certainty, along with gospel parallels.

Fragment I verso

```
. . . . . .
. . . to the lawyers
. . . every transgressor
. . . and not me . . .
5   . . . how he does . . . to
(the) rulers of the people
. . . he said this word, Search
the scriptures, in which you
suppose you have life; they are
```

John 5:39: Search the scriptures, for you suppose that in them you have eternal life; they are those which

10 those which testify about me;
do not suppose that I came to
accuse you to my Father; there
is Moses who accuses you, on
whom you have set your hope.
15 When they said, We know well
that to Moses God spoke, but
we do not know you . . . Jesus
answered and said to them,
Now is accused your unbelief
. . .

testify about me. 5:45: Do not suppose that I will accuse you to the
Father; there is one who accuses
you, Moses, on whom you have set
your hope. 9:29: We know that God
spoke to Moses, but as for this man,
we do not know whence he is.

cf. John 9:41, 12:31, 3:18

Fragment I recto

. . . to the crowd . . .
. . . stones together to stone
him; and they laid
25 their hands on him, the rulers,
to take him and . . .
to the crowd; and they could
not take him because not yet
had come his hour of betrayal.
30 But the Lord himself, going
out . . .
. . . departed from them.
And behold, a leper coming to
him, says, Teacher Jesus, while
35 traveling and eating with lepers
in the inn I became a leper my-
self; if then . . .
I am cleansed. The Lord . . .
I wish, be cleansed . . .
40 The leprosy left him.
. . . Go, (show yourself) to the
(priests)

John 8:59: They took up stones to
cast at him

7:30: they sought to take him

his hour was not yet come

cf. Matt. 8:2–3; Mark 1:40–2;
Luke 5:12–13

no gospel parallel

Matt. 8:3; Mark 1:42
cf. Mark 1:42

'as a testimony to them'; 'priests' in
Luke 17:14[1]

Fragment II recto

. . . to him they (asked him)
testing him (saying),
45 Teacher Jesus, we know that . . .
you have come, for what you
do (bears witness) beyond all
the prophets . . .
to us: is it right to kings . . .
50 what pertains to authority? . . .
to them or not? But Jesus,
knowing their mind, was indignant and said to them, Why
do you call me with your
55 mouth Teacher and do not
hear what I say? Well, did
(Isaiah) prophesy about you,
saying, this people honor me
with their lips but their heart is

cf. Matt. 22:15–16 and parallels

John 3:2: Rabbi, we know that you
have come as a teacher from God;
for no one can do the signs . . .

Matt. 22:17; Mark 12:14; Luke
20:22

Mark 1:43: indignant (cf. John
11:33). Luke 6:46: Why do you call
me Lord, Lord, and do not do what
I say? Matt. 15:7–9; Mark 7:6–7:
Well did Isaiah prophesy, etc.

1 On the textual variants in the synoptics see G. Mayeda, *Das
Leben-Jesu-Fragment Papyrus Egerton 2* (Bern, 1946), 36.

60 far from me; in vain they worship me, commandments . . .

Fragment II verso

. . . to the place with closed   no gospel parallels
. . . is subject unclearly
. . . his weight unweighed . . .
65 . . . they were perplexed
at the strange question
. . . walking, Jesus stood
at the mouth of the Jordan
river and stretching forth his
70 right hand . . .
. . . and sowed on the
. . . and then . . .
. . . water . . .
. . . and . . .
75 . . . brought forth fruit . . .
. . . much . . .

The first point to be made about this combination of
various kinds of materials is that they come from what we
know as Johannine, synoptic, and apocryphal. Fragment I
verso is almost entirely Johannine; I recto begins with
Johannine motifs and continues with a variant version of a
synoptic story; II recto combines two synoptic-type
pericopes and uses some Johannine phrasing; and II verso
seems to contain an apocryphal miracle-story. (By 'synoptic'
we mean primarily Matthaean and Marcan, for the parallels
to Luke provided by the first editors depend partly on the
way in which they have filled in gaps in the text; but the
parallel in lines 52–4 is rather striking.)

The second point is that the order we have given is not
necessarily correct. Another possibility, as Bell and Skeat
point out, is that II verso may have come first, with II recto
(and a reference to what Jesus is doing) following it; later
in the book, but probably still in the first half of it, would
come I verso and recto. The sequence of the gospel parallels
to the fragments gives us little, if any, aid.

The third point is that the parallels are remarkably close
to (though usually not identical with) the Gospel of John.
Fragment I verso begins with something very close to John

5:39 and substitutes 'life' (as in John 5:40) for 'eternal life'. Next comes the equivalent of John 5:45, with 'I came' inserted from John 5:43. The mention of Moses leads on to John 9:29 (as Jeremias suggested[1]), and Jesus' answer recalls three other Johannine passages (9:41, 12:31, 3:18). In I recto we begin with something like John 8:59 (10:31) and go on to John 7:30 (32, 44; 8:20). The Johannine 'hour' is explained as the 'hour of betrayal' as in Mark 14:41. Then, after Jesus leaves the rulers (as in John 8:59 and 10:39), we find the story of a leper—a variant of that told in Mark 1:40–45 and parallels (see also Luke 17:11–19, another variant?). Fragment II recto begins with the synoptic question about paying tribute, but there are striking differences from Mark 12:13–17 and parallels. Mark's story of their question has them begin with the words, 'Teacher, we know that you are true'. Our fragment, however, seems much closer to John 3:2, where Nicodemus (a 'ruler of the Jews') says, 'Rabbi, we know that you have come as a teacher from God, for no one can do these signs which you do unless God is with him.' And the question itself deals not with Caesar but with 'kings', not with tribute but with 'what pertains to their authority'. Jesus is then 'indignant', as in Mark's story of the leper (1:43), and calls for true understanding (= obedience) as in Luke 6:46. With this is combined a statement about the prophecy of Isaiah 29:13, phrased much as in Matthew 15:7–9 and Mark 7:6–7.

What are we to make of this? One point is very clear: the author of the 'unknown gospel' did not make *direct* use of our gospels, in the sense that he transcribed them word for word into his own book. Instead, it is practically certain that he was relying on his memory, and that his memory did not provide verbal exactitude. But this certainty only opens the way to a further question: is the 'unknown gospel' based

1 Cf. Mayeda, *op. cit.*, 66.

on memories of (a) the written gospels (John and some, at least, of the synoptics), or (b) oral traditions, or (c) both kinds of materials? Here it would appear that the latest conclusion of C. H. Dodd has much to commend it: 'although I believe that in the first fragment of Pap. Eg. 2 there is a direct quotation from the Fourth Gospel, I now think it more probable that fragment 2 is a divergent rendering of a common tradition all through (as it pretty clearly is in its main substance).'[1] This is to say that the fragments reflect a situation not unlike that depicted by Papias—one in which books (e.g., Mark or John) are certainly in circulation, but oral tradition is still very highly valued; and the two kinds of sources obviously overlap.

It is the kind of situation to which Koester points in his book on synoptic tradition; though written gospels were in existence, not all the Apostolic Fathers made direct use of them. Only the passage of time, and the increasing danger of Gnostic secret traditions, could drive most of the oral traditions out of general circulation.

This situation means that we encounter grave difficulties when we try to describe or analyse the period of transition. When an early Christian writer is quoting a saying of Jesus, for example, he may do so in a variety of ways. (1) He may be copying it out of a book; this situation is likely to exist if a long selection is being used. (2) He may be quoting from memory what he has read in a book. (3) He may be quoting from memory what he has heard from someone else—and his informant can have derived the information either from (a) a book or from (b) oral tradition. Unfortunately it is not always or, indeed, often possible to determine which one of these possibilities is the actuality, or whether any one is the actuality rather than a combination of several of them.

1 C. H. Dodd, *Historical Tradition in the Fourth Gospel* (Cambridge, 1963), 329.

Our negative conclusion is reinforced by the ways in which some, though not all, early Christian writers give quotations from the Old Testament and from the Pauline epistles. In these situations they are obviously relying upon written documents; but in the Gospel of John there are almost never exact quotations and in I Clement there is a mixture of exact quotations and highly inexact ones. The letters of Ignatius, as we have seen, are crowded with reminiscences of the Pauline epistles, especially I Corinthians; but Ignatius never provides explicit quotations from them.

This means that among early Christian writers there is a considerable measure of freedom in the citing of authoritative texts. They are concerned not with the letter but with the spirit of the texts and of the oral traditions as well. And when the authors of the New Testament apocrypha makes use either of texts or of traditions they are undoubtedly convinced that they are entitled to the same freedom. Only the gradual exaltation of the texts regarded as alone authoritative, along with the gradual development of the limits of doctrinal variety, made it possible for the Church as a whole to reject the apocryphal writings.

VIII

The New Testament books in Gnostic circles

In tracing the usage and the authority of the New Testament books in the second century we obviously cannot limit our investigation to the writings of those whom the 'great Church' then or later regarded as orthodox. We must also consider the extant fragments of the works of important heretics such as Basilides, Marcion, and Valentinus (with his disciples). These fragments clearly show the way in which their authors viewed the New Testament writings, and they provide invaluable supplements to the more orthodox treatments which we shall discuss in Chapters IX and X.

The reason for regarding these Gnostics' writings so highly is that they considered themselves to be Christians. In most instances, they did not intend to break away from the Church; they remained within it until they were expelled, and in some instances—perhaps in the case of Basilides— they were not in fact expelled. Their writings are likely to be based upon ordinary Christian usage at the times, and in the places, in which they wrote.

Basilides

The earliest and most important witness is Basilides, who taught at Alexandria during the reign of Trajan (A.D. 117–

138). Here the question is whether we can or cannot rely upon the account of his teaching provided by Hippolytus in a book (the *Refutation of Heresies*) written in the third century. P. Hendrix, followed by other scholars, has cogently argued that Hippolytus preserves the authentic teaching of Basilides and that conflicting accounts of it provided by other authors are secondary.[1] Since this is the case, we cannot agree with E. Jacquier that the formulas of citation in Hippolytus' account come from Hippolytus rather than from Basilides.[2] Our case is supported by the statement of Agrippa Castor (second century) that Basilides wrote twenty-four books of *Exegetica* on the Gospel.[3] According to a quotation from them in the *Acta Archelai*, Basilides ascribed the parable of Dives and Lazarus (Luke 16:19–31) to 'the saving Word'.[4]

It is therefore extremely significant that in Hippolytus' account of the system we find exegesis of John, Luke, and Matthew—introduced by formulas identical with the ones Basilides uses in relation to Old Testament texts. 'This is what the gospels mean when they say' (John 1:9; Hippolytus, *Ref.* 7, 22, 4); 'this is what is meant by' (Luke 1:35; 7, 26, 9); 'this is proved by the Savior's saying' (John 2:4; 7, 27, 5) . . . 'as well as by the Magi who saw the star' (Matt. 2:1–2; *ibid.*).

Even more striking is the way in which Basilides refers to the Pauline epistles. He used the formula 'as it is written' in referring to texts from Romans (7, 25, 1–2), 2 Corinthians,

1 *De Alexandrijnsche Haeresiarch Basilides* (Amsterdam, 1926); cf. J. H. Waszink, 'Basilides', *Reallexikon für Antike und Christentum* I, 1217–25.

2 *Le Nouveau Testament dans l'Eglise chrétienne* I (ed. 2, Paris, 1911), 146–48.

3 Eusebius, *H. E.* 4, 7, 7.

4 Translations in R. M. Grant, *Gnosticism: an Anthology* (London-New York, 1961), 123–37.

Ephesians (7, 26, 7). Indeed, he cites 1 Corinthians 2:13 with the formula 'the scripture says' (7, 25, 3). Jacquier argues that 'it would be remarkable, if Basilides really used these formulas, for him to be the first writer to attest the divine authority of the New Testament books'.[1] But, as he himself points out, we find something similar in the Epistle of Barnabas—and, we should add, in Polycarp and 2 Clement. We conclude that Basilides only makes explicit what other Christians already implicitly held, and that he is a witness to Alexandrian Christian usage in his time.

It is often supposed that (1) the New Testament books were not regarded as scripture until at least the middle of the second century, and that (2) the impetus for so regarding them was given by Marcion of Pontus, who taught at Rome between 137 and 144. If we now recognize that at Alexandria some New Testament books were already regarded as scripture, we cannot give Marcion quite as high marks as he has usually received, and we must give due weight to the possibility—one might better say, probability—that the idea of treating New Testament books as 'scripture' arose in Alexandria early in the second century.

There are good historical grounds for supposing that this was the case. Among Alexandrian Gnostics and, one may perhaps infer, among those Alexandrian Christians who were more 'orthodox', there was usually considerable reverence for the Old Testament—at least as interpreted allegorically. This point of view may have been, though we cannot say definitely that it was, reflected in such documents as Hebrews and Barnabas. Suppose one were to jettison the Old Testament? Suppose one were to believe that the Christian revelation was new, even if one did not jettison the Old Testament? In either case one would tend to apply to the New Testament documents the honorific titles already

1 *Op. cit.*, 147.

used in regard to Old Testament books. And this is the situation we encounter in the remains of Basilides' works.

This is to say—as Jacquier refused to say—that the earliest witness to a definite view of the New Testament writings as 'scripture' is the Alexandrian Gnostic Basilides. We should also, however, in part reject what Jacquier rejected: the notion that Gnostics led the way in this regard. We should do so partly because of our previous interpretation of the Apostolic Fathers as on the verge of viewing the New Testament books as scripture but either reluctant to do so or not interested in the question. We should also do so because at Alexandria and elsewhere Gnosticism was so close to 'orthodox' Christian ideas. The fact that Basilides is our first clear witness to the idea that New Testament writings were 'scripture' does not prove that he was the first to hold this view. In fact, the rather offhand way in which he so speaks of them suggests that he shared the idea with others, and that Alexandrian 'orthodox' Christians— about whom we know nothing—may well have held the same opinion. We can, however, definitely infer from Basilides' statements that it was at Alexandria that the idea of treating the New Testament books as scripture first arose; and it should be added that the New Testament books included at least three gospels (Basilides may not mention Mark because it was being regarded as secret; see Chapter XI) and four Pauline epistles—therefore probably more. Indeed, the evidence which Basilides supplies suggests that we should go farther still in creating hypotheses, and perhaps should argue that 2 Peter (see Chapter I) may as well be from Alexandria as anywhere else.

Marcion

This leaves us with the question of what Marcion contributed. Especially during the last century, scholars have often argued that he was responsible for creating the canon of the New Testament. The grounds for this judgment are fairly solid. Marcion wrote a book of *Antitheses* in which he contrasted his own ethical dualism, as based on New Testament texts, with other (inferior) New Testament texts and on passages from the Old Testament. His basic idea was that there were two gods: one the good Father of Jesus, the other the just (and sometimes bad) creator-god of the Old Testament. Given this starting point he could proceed to publish the authentic *Gospel* (Luke, without interpolations) and *Apostle* (Paul, without interpolations and without the Pastoral Epistles). His ideas about authenticity seem to have been based on a combination of some textual evidence with a great deal of confidence that he alone knew what the gospel should have been and what Paul should have written. The theory of interpolations, rather fashionable in his day,[1] allowed for a considerable exercise of ingenuity, especially —as presented by Marcion—without any supporting evidence. Somehow, as Irenaeus remarked, 'he persuaded his disciples that he was more trustworthy than the apostles who transmitted the gospel'.[2]

In preparing his *Apostle*, Marcion apparently arranged the letters in relation to length—except for Galatians, which he viewed as most important because it was opposed to Judaizers and showed Paul rebuking Peter. He therefore placed this letter first and continued with Corinthians I–II, Romans, Thessalonians I–II, Ephesians (which he called

1 See *The Letter and the Spirit* (London, 1957), 21–25.
2 *Gnosticism: an Anthology*, 45.

'Laodiceans', presumably because of the mention of the letter from Laodicea in Colossians 4:16), Colossians–Philemon, and Philippians.[1] There is some chronological arrangement here, for the imprisonment epistles come at the end; but the place of the Thessalonian letters does not seem right. Since Marcion did not accept Acts, he was deprived of the assistance it gives toward arranging the Pauline epistles—and also did not have to face some of the difficulties involved.

What was his contribution? It seems to have consisted not so much of the idea of a canon, or of the creation of a canon, as of the rigorous and rather misguided principles on the basis of which he produced his works. It is true, however, that his method and results forced more orthodox Christians to examine their own presuppositions and to state more clearly what they already believed.

The Valentinians

Marcion was not the only heretic who flourished at Rome in the middle of the second century. Around the same time, and somewhat later as well, there was an equally important Gnostic teacher named Valentinus, along with his principal disciple, Ptolemaeus. From the fragments of Valentinus' writings we cannot determine how he viewed the New Testament books. Van Unnik has shown that *if* he wrote the so-called *Gospel of Truth* he probably knew a rather extensive New Testament collection with Hebrews though apparently without the Pastoral Epistles.[2] Since we are not sure that he

---

1 See J. Knox, *Marcion and the New Testament* (Chicago, 1942), 40–46.

2 W. C. van Unnik in F. L. Cross (ed.), *The Jung Codex* (London, 1955).

did write the *Gospel of Truth*, we turn to the fragments of Ptolemaeus. These fragments show that Ptolemaeus regard-ed the New Testament books—properly interpreted—as supremely authoritative because they contained the apostolic tradition which came from the Savior Jesus. He never uses the word 'scripture'; instead, he speaks of what 'the Savior said' or did and refers to 'the sayings of Jesus'. These are contained in the gospels of Matthew, Mark, and Luke; though Ptolemaeus certainly knew the Gospel of John, we cannot tell how he viewed the sayings contained in it. As for the epistles, he uses only Romans, 1–2 Corinthians, Gala-tians, Ephesians, and Colossians, usually speaking of them as written by Paul or 'the apostle', although once he gives a more specific reference: 'Paul said in First Corinthians' (this is the earliest example of such precision). He describes the Fourth Gospel as written by 'John the Lord's disciple', and refers to him, as to Paul, as 'the apostle'.[1] This evidence clearly shows that like Marcion the Valentinians venerated Paul; unlike him they also used John and the other synoptics. They were closer to the Church as a whole than Marcion was, at least in this respect.

Ptolemaeus also wrote a brief commentary on the prologue to the Gospel of John, and somewhat later another Valen-tinian named Heracleon composed exegetical notes on parts, at least, of the first eight chapters of the Gospel. These notes, known to us from Origen's *Commentary on John*, reveal the mind of a subtle allegorizer, interpreting what Jesus 'really' meant when his disciple John was recording his words. Heracleon makes use of Matthew, Romans, 1 Corinthians, Hebrews, Revelation—and the apocryphal *Preaching of Peter*, which, like Clement of Alexandria (Chapter XI), he viewed as authentic.

Ptolemaeus and Heracleon represent the 'western' wing of

1 See *Gnosticism: an Anthology*, 162–90.

Valentinianism, and it is therefore important to observe that their use of documents the Church in the West regarded as apocryphal was much more restrained than was the use we find reflected in the remains of works by the Eastern Theodotus and Marcus. Theodotus, from whose writings Clement of Alexandria compiled excerpts, relies on three classes of authorities: (1) the prophets, inspired by the Spirit, who wrote 'the prophetic writings' of the Old Testament (individuals wrote 'the word of the prophet' or 'the prophecy'); (2) the Savior, who taught the apostles in three ways (in prefigurations and mysteries, in parables and enigmas, and plainly and unveiledly); and (3) the apostles, the most important of whom was Paul.[1] The formulas Theodotus uses in providing references are like those we have found in Ptolemaeus.

'the Savior says' or 'said' 'the Lord said'	four gospels; perhaps also *Egyptians* (67, 2)
'the apostle says' or 'said'	Paul or John; also Luke (74, 2)
'it is said'	Ephesians (41, 2); synoptic tradition (42,3); perhaps *Thomas* (21, 3)
'the passage' or 'the saying' (Greek word *to* without a noun)	Genesis (21, 1); Deuteronomy (28); also John (6, 1)
no formula	Pauline expressions; Proverbs (47, 1); Daniel (38, 1); Mark (85, 1)

Theodotus thus treats his Old and New Testament authorities alike. His New Testament seems to be considerably more extensive than that of Ptolemaeus, if (and the 'if' is important) he derived non-canonical sayings of Jesus from

1 Clement, *Exc. Theod.* 24, 1; 50, 3; 47, 3; 62, 2; 66.

books. Like Ptolemaeus, he had a collection of Pauline epistles; in his discussions we find echoes from Romans, 1 Corinthians, Galatians, Ephesians, Philippians, and Colossians.

The Valentinians who followed Marcus were farther from the main stream of Catholic Christianity. According to Irenaeus, they used 'a multitude of apocryphal and spurious writings which they themselves forged'. Among these was a tradition about how the boy Jesus taught his teacher; they also used at least one saying of Jesus which we find in the *Gospel of Thomas*.[1]

None of the Valentinians seems to have employed the word 'scripture', and this silence can be explained in various ways. First, of course, and probably most important is the fact that for them what mattered was not the written word as such but what it mysteriously signified. Second, they may have avoided the term 'scripture' because at the time when they began to separate from the Church it was not commonly used in regard to New Testament books and, indeed, in their own time was not often employed. They would have noticed that when Paul and other New Testament writers speak of 'scripture' they are referring to the Old Testament. The view of Basilides, as we have observed, is different from that of the Valentinians.

Generally speaking, Gnostic usage strongly resembles what we have already encountered among the Apostolic Fathers. Basilides knew at least three gospels and treated them as he treated Old Testament texts; he viewed at least four Pauline epistles as 'scripture' (Romans, 1–2 Corinthians, Ephesians). Marcion used only one gospel (Luke, revised version) and ten Pauline epistles. The Valentinians generally relied on four gospels, although they also made use of traditions found in the *Gospel of the Egyptians* and the

1 Irenaeus, *Adv. haer.* 1, 20, 1–2.

E

Gospel of Thomas. All our Valentinian witnesses made use of Romans and 1 Corinthians; two of them employ Galatians, Ephesians, and Colossians; 2 Corinthians and Philippians also appear.

It is probably significant that the Valentinians, who did not use the term 'scripture' of New Testament writings, stood rather close to Jewish Christianity and, indeed, to heterodox Judaism, while Basilides and Marcion more clearly reflect gentile ideas. This difference corresponds with what we have already found in the Apostolic Fathers. The movement toward the creation of a New Testament was due to gentile Christians, orthodox and unorthodox alike.

IX

The New Testament books
in the Greek Apologists

Justin

With the writings of the apologist Justin (*c.* 150—*c.* 160) we first encounter Christianity as presented by a self-conscious literary creator, a man acquainted with the protocol of presenting petitions to the emperor and with the dialogue form, and able to provide allusions to Greek poetry and quotations from Plato. Because of Justin's literary environment and intention, we should expect him to have an idea of the New Testament books as literature and to express it somewhat more clearly than did the Apostolic Fathers. This is all the more likely since he presents Old Testament quotations only from the books recognized by Jews as canonical (see Chapter II)—even though he uses a version rather different from the ordinary Septuagint text.

When he says, as we shall see, that what the Christians call 'gospels' can be classified as 'reminiscences' or 'memoranda' (*Apol.* 1, 66, 3), he is presumably trying to explain to Greek readers the degree to which they resemble Xenophon's *Memorabilia of Socrates*—a work which he describes but does not name (*Apol.* 2, 11, 3). This fact suggests that in trying to understand his ideas about a canon (if he had one) we must bear in mind that his extant works are addressed to those outside the Church. He is not necessarily setting forth all he knows, and what he does set forth is not necessarily expressed in language always characteristic of the Christian community.

When we speak of language characteristic of the Christian community, however, we must bear in mind that this language was not something fixed or clearly differentiated from Hellenistic Greek in general. Similarly, the attitude of early Christians toward books as such, scriptural or non-scriptural, was not uniform. Those who like Justin were accustomed to deal with Greek books and to cite them or their authors by name followed the same practise in citing biblical writings. More precisely, those early Christians such as the Apostolic Fathers who do not explicitly refer to Greek literary work are not likely to provide exact references to the books of the Old Testament or the New; Justin, on the other hand, provides fairly exact references for his quotations not only from the biblical books but also from the *Timaeus* of Plato (*Apol.* 1, 60, 1; *Dial.* 5, 4), the Socratic dialogues (*Apol.* 2, 3, 6; 2, 10, 5–6), and the writings of Xenophon. To be sure, Justin's references are not always exact. As in modern times, in antiquity it was not always necessary to point precisely to one's sources, even if one knew what they were. A quotation from the *Republic* of Plato in *Apology* 1, 3, 3 is introduced by the rather vague and rather elegant expression, 'One of the ancients said somewhere'; and in *Apology* 1, 39, 4 a line from Euripides is called 'what is said'. In *Dialogue* 1, 3 Justin addresses Trypho with a tag from the *Iliad*; 'I addressed him jestingly', he says, thus indicating that both Trypho and the reader of the *Dialogue* were expected to recognize the allusion.

We should not claim that there is a mathematically demonstrable correlation between an author's exact citations from

Greek literature and his exact citations from biblical writings. In general, however, something of a correlation does exist, and it shows that the question of canonicity is to some extent a cultural question as well as a theological one. It is not an accident, we suggest, that the canonical books come clearly into light, that attempts are made to delimit the canon precisely among those writers who stand closest to Graeco-Roman literary culture—i.e., Clement, Origen, and Eusebius (see Chapter XI), and that the clearest evidence from an earlier time occurs in the writings of the Gnostics who are sometimes expressing their ideas in relation to Hellenistic philosophy and theology (Chapter VIII).

Because Justin was writing in a period crucial for our understanding of the use of the New Testament, we should pay very close attention to the differences and similarities between what he says in his earlier *Apology* (about A.D. 150) and what he says in his later *Dialogue with Trypho* (about 160). During the decade between the two works Justin's own ideas, not to mention those held in the Roman community, may well have undergone some changes.

Some of the ideas are definitely the same. For instance, in the *Apology* (1, 28, 1) he says that 'from our writings' (i.e., those of the Christians) readers can learn that Christians call the chief of the demons by the names 'serpent', 'Satan', and 'devil'. The same point is made with greater precision in the *Dialogue* (103, 5). Moses (i.e., in Genesis) calls him 'serpent', Job and Zechariah call him 'devil', and Jesus calls him 'Satan'. Thus it becomes clear that Justin has in mind the synoptic gospels, where Jesus uses this name. Again, in the *Apology* (66, 3; 67, 3) Justin twice refers to the 'memoranda' or 'reminiscences' of the apostles, which he identifies, in the latter passage, by the Christian name 'gospels'. These books contain accounts of what Jesus did and said, and like the writings of the prophets, they are read aloud at Christian worship. The same terms recur in the *Dialogue* although, oddly enough, the 'memoranda' are mentioned only in chapters 100–07, chiefly in relation to exegesis of the Christological Psalm 21 (22). For this reason W. Bousset offered the conjecture that Justin was making use of an earlier commentary he had written on this psalm—and he was probably right.[1] Both in the *Apology* and in the *Dialogue* Justin's primary authority is the Old Testament.

On the other hand, there are some differences between the two works. The additions, some of them explanatory or exegetical, which Justin makes to the gospel narratives in the *Apology* are few and far between, while in the *Dialogue* (especially in cc. 78 and 88) they are much more common. At the same time, Justin has learned, doubtless from controversy, something about quoting from texts. In the *Apology* he was content to quote 'verbatim' from Genesis (32, 1; 59, 1) and Isaiah (33, 1). By the time he wrote the *Dialogue* he was aware that there were various versions of the Old Testament in Greek, and he refers to differences among them no fewer than seven times (71–73; 120; 124; 137–38).[2] A similar movement toward exactness also occurs in relation to the gospels. In the *Apology* (34, 2) he had wrongly stated that Quirinius was the first procurator of Judaea; in the *Dialogue* (78, 4) he more accurately states that the first census took place under Quirinius (Luke 2:2). And only in the *Dialogue* do we find exact statements about what 'is written in the memoranda of the apostles' (100–1; 103–4; 106–7). It is there that we also find a statement which shows how these memoranda were at least on the verge of being regarded as scripture. In *Dialogue* 49, 5 Justin begins by

1 *Jüdisch-christlicher Schulbetrieb in Alexandreia und Rom* (Göttingen, 1915), 292–93.

2 On a text not unlike his see D. Barthélemy in *Revue Biblique* 60 (1953), 18–29.

quoting what 'our Christ' said; these are the words found in
Matthew 17:10–12a. Immediately afterwards he proceeds
thus: 'And it is written that, Then the disciples understood
that he spoke to them about John the Baptist' (Matt. 17:13).
'It is written' is doubtless equivalent to 'it is written in the
memoranda of the apostles'; but since in the *Dialogue*
Justin has not yet referred to these memoranda (and the
passage occurs before the point at which there is a break in
the manuscript), it is more than likely that he is using the
formula ordinarily employed in regard to Old Testament
books in relation to the gospels. After all, as we have already
seen, the gospels were included with the Old Testament
books among 'our writings'.[1]

The movement toward precision reflected in the *Dialogue*
also suggests that we should take seriously what he says
about the authors of the memoranda: these books were
composed by 'the apostles and by those who followed them'
(103, 8). This statement may be based, at least verbally, on
the preface to Luke's gospel, where we find the same word
for 'follow' and a similar word for 'compose' (Luke 1:1, 3).
In addition, Justin soon afterwards refers to a statement
found only in Mark 3:16–17 and locates it in the 'memoranda of Peter' (106, 3). This means that we cannot neatly
differentiate apostolic and sub-apostolic gospels in Justin's
usage. He is ascribing a book by a disciple of an apostle to
the apostle himself. It remains likely, however, that he knew
the sub-apostolic gospels ascribed to Luke and Mark and,
to judge from his other quotations, the apostolic gospels
ascribed to Matthew and John.

It is odd that there is only one rather clear quotation from

1 It is probable that Justin knew the book of Acts; cf. F. Overbeck
in *Zeitschrift für Wissenschaftliche Theologie* 15 (1872), 305–49, for an
inconclusive attempt to prove that he did. A more conclusive proof is
provided by E. Haenchen, *Die Apostelgeschichte* (Göttingen, 1959), 6–7.
The primary text is *Apol.* 1, 50, 12 (Acts 1:8).

John (3:3, 5) in his writings (*Apol.* 1, 64, 1): 'Christ said, "Unless you are born again you will not enter into the kingdom of heaven." ' This reticence is rather surprising in view of his explicit statement (*Dial.* 81, 4) that the book of Revelation was written by John, one of the apostles of Christ. From this book Justin derived not only his millenarian views but also—though he does not say so—the statement we have already mentioned, that the chief of the evil demons is called 'serpent and Satan and devil' (*Apol.* 1, 28, 1; *Dial.* 103, 5; 125, 4). We have no reason to suppose that Justin viewed the author of Revelation as also the author of the Gospel; perhaps he knew the latter work (if, indeed, he knew it) as anonymous but somehow apostolic.

Another difficulty arises when we consider the Gospel of Luke. Presumably Justin thought it was written by a disciple of an apostle. If so, the apostle must have been Paul—whose letters he never quotes. Perhaps this situation was due to controversy at Rome over Marcion's collection of Pauline epistles. Furthermore, Justin's extant works were written for non-Christian audiences. He could not appeal to the authority of the Pauline epistles without raising the problem of Paul's place in Christianity. Finally, the Pauline epistles themselves were addressed to Christians, not to outsiders. Perhaps he thought it would be unsuitable to use them.

Justin's 'New Testament', it would appear, consisted of 'gospels' or 'memoranda' written by apostles and their followers, and of the book of Revelation. If we possessed books he wrote for Christian readers we might well find that he regarded the Pauline epistles as authoritative as well—perhaps also 1 Peter and 1 John—but we do not possess such books.

In addition, he made use of various traditions, probably oral, about the life of Jesus. These resemble the midrashic additions he sometimes makes to the Old Testament and do not affect his 'canon' one way or the other. It is clear, however, that such traditions were sometimes authoritative for him. In the *Dialogue* (47, 5) he states that 'our Lord Jesus Christ said, "In what I find you, in this will I judge you" '. This quotation does not occur in the four gospels; it is found as an oral tradition in a sermon by Clement of Alexandria.[1] At least implicitly, then, Justin recognizes the authority of oral tradition as well as that of written books.

Tatian

The situation is somewhat different when we turn to Justin's sometime disciple Tatian, who composed his *Oration to the Greeks* about 176. Justin had often mentioned Jesus and, as we have seen, had spoken of the gospels and Revelation. Tatian never explicitly mentions Jesus and never refers precisely to any New Testament books. He likes to be mysterious, as a semi-Gnostic passage in the *Oration* (*c.* 30) shows; but there he does not refer to the Matthaean parables for which he is supplying allegorical exegesis or, for that matter, to the Gnostic gospels of Thomas and Philip to which his thought is close.[2] In *Oration* 13 he refers to John 1:5 as 'what is said' but does not tell his reader who said it, and in *Oration* 19 he quotes John 1:3 exactly but does not indicate that he is quoting. In chapter 15 there is an explicit but inaccurate quotation from Psalm 8:6 'in accordance with the word which says . . .'

On the other hand, there are frequent allusions to the Pauline epistles—especially, it would appear, to Romans, 1–2 Corinthians, Galatians, Colossians, and either Ephesians

---

1 *Quis div. salv.* 40, 2.
2 See *Journal of Theological Studies* 15 (1964), 65–69.

or 1 Thessalonians—as well as to Hebrews. From the fragmentary remains of other works we know that he provided exegesis of 1 Corinthians, Galatians, and Romans. His collection of New Testament books thus closely resembled that of his contemporary, the Valentinian Heracleon (see Chapter V).[1]

According to Jerome he rejected 'some epistles of Paul' but recognized the authority of the letter to Titus (*In Ep. ad Tit.*, praef.). Such recognition may conceivably be due to certain points at which Tatian could find theological support in Titus; the word 'continent' (*encratēs*) occurs in Titus 1:7, and Tatian was the leader of the Encratite heresy.

His most important work was the *Diatessaron*, in which he wove together the content of the four canonical gospels, possibly also (like Justin) making use of some oral traditions. The title shows that Tatian obviously recognized the primacy and uniqueness of only four gospels.[2]

Melito

Another Christian apologist of the later second century was Melito of Sardis, whose extensive writings are lost except for a few fragments and a paschal sermon preserved in Greek and Coptic and summarized in Latin.[3] Unfortunately for our purposes, nothing that survives contains any reference to New Testament books. Melito was certainly concerned with the Old Testament. In the sermon he quotes from Moses, David, Jeremiah, and Isaiah; and it begins with the

1 See *Texte und Untersuchungen* 63 (1957), 297–306.

2 See *The Earliest Lives of Jesus* (London–New York, 1961), 22–28.

3 See 'The Fragments of the Greek Apologists and Irenaeus' in J. N. Birdsall–R. W. Thomson, *Biblical and Patristic Studies in Memory of R. P. Casey* (Freiburg, 1963), 192–201.

words, 'The scripture of the Hebrew Exodus has been read and the words of the mystery have been explained, how the sheep is sacrificed and how the people is delivered.' Echoes of New Testament expressions are fairly common, but Melito does not tell us how he viewed the books.

We have already seen (Chapter II) that he was eager to find out the exact contents of the Old Testament; he listed 'the old books', i.e. 'the books of the old covenant'. It has sometimes been argued that he must have known the expression 'New Testament', but this is not logically implied by what he said. What is implied is that he knew of 'new books' corresponding with old ones, and of 'books of the new covenant' corresponding with books of the old one.

Though Melito is not a witness to a New Testament as such, he is a witness to the exaltation of the New Testament books among gentile Christians. Like Ignatius, he is a representative of the Hellenistic culture, deeply influenced by rhetoric, with which Christians were becoming acquainted in the second century.[1]

Athenagoras

The apologist Athenagoras, who wrote his *Legatio* about the year 178 perhaps at Alexandria, makes explicit use of writings contained in the Old and New Testaments.[2] He refers to the divine inspiration of Moses, Isaiah, Jeremiah, and 'the rest of the prophets', and provides quotations from Baruch (3:36) and Isaiah (44:6; 43:10–11; 66:1), referring his imperial addressees to the books which contain the

[1] On Melito's style see A. Wifstrand in *Vigiliae Christianae* 2 (1948), 201–23.

[2] Sections numbered in accordance with the edition of P. Ubaldi–M. Pellegrino (Torino, 1947).

prophecies (9, 1–3). He ascribes two quotations from Proverbs to 'the prophetic Spirit' (10, 4; 18, 2), and in the first instance adds that 'we declare that the Holy Spirit . . . is an emanation from God, emanating and returning like a ray of the sun'—an allusion to Wisdom 7:25. Two of Athenagoras' references to the Sermon on the Mount contain statements that Christians have learned these words or were bought up on them (1, 4; 11, 2). He quotes various verses in a form in which the Matthaean and the Lucan versions are blended together (1, 4; 12, 3) but sometimes follows Matthew alone (11, 2; 32, 2) or what looks like Mark (33, 5).[1] There seem to be allusions to John in his statements about the Son's being in the Father and the Father in the Son (10, 2) and about Roman rule as given 'from above' (18, 2; John 19, 11).

There are indisputable allusions to Romans 1:27 (34, 2), Galatians 4:9 (16, 3), and 1 Timothy 2:1–2 (37, 2–3); these show that Athenagoras possessed a collection of Pauline epistles, including the Pastorals, but do not allow us to say how he regarded them.

As for the treatise *On the Resurrection of the Dead* ascribed to him, we find in it definite quotations from God's law in Exodus (23, 2–5) and statements 'according to the apostle' based on 1 Corinthians 15:53 and 2 Corinthians 5:10 (18, 5). In both the *Legatio* (12, 3) and the treatise (19, 3) there is probably an allusion to 1 Corinthians 15:32.

A quotation from 'the word which says' (*Leg.* 32, 5) comes from a manual of church discipline, not from something like the Old or New Testament.

---

1 Matt. 5:28, 5:39–40 with Luke 6:29, 5:44–45, 5:46a plus Luke 6:34a plus Matt. 5:46b; Mark 10:11.

Theophilus

Somewhere around the year 180, and a bit later, the bishop Theophilus of Antioch addressed three apologetic treatises to a certain Autolycus. These books contain allusions to all four gospels and possibly to Acts, to all the Pauline epistles except 1–2 Thessalonians, and to Hebrews, 1 Peter, 1 John, and Revelation. His 'canon' thus contains the books which were later accepted at Antioch (see Chapter X).

In addition, Theophilus provides explicit quotations from two gospels and three epistles. These quotations occur in two sections which deserve to be reproduced almost in full. First, in *Ad Autolycum* 2, 22 he speaks of the generation of the Word and points out that it is taught us by 'the holy scriptures and all the inspired men, one of whom, John, says, "In the beginning was the Word, and the Word was before God"—showing that originally God was alone and the Word was in him'. Theophilus then continues his quotation with these words: 'And the Word was God; everything came into existence through him, and apart from him nothing came into existence.' This passage clearly shows that Theophilus regarded John as inspired like the Old Testament prophets and, for that matter, the Sibyl (2, 9). Since he views John's teaching as derived from the Spirit of God, the Gospel must be as authoritative as any Old Testament book. It must be equivalent to scripture, whether Theophilus says so or not. We should also point out that in his view John wrote a gospel. Theophilus therefore is not making use of Tatian's *Diatessaron* but of an individual gospel-book.

Second, in *Ad Autolycum* 3, 13–14 Theophilus quotes passages (perhaps against Marcion's *Antitheses*) to show that there is a synthesis of the prophets and the gospel.

Concerning chastity the holy Word teaches us not to sin, not only in deed but even in thought, not to think in one's heart about any evil or to desire another's wife when one has beheld her. Now Solomon, who was a king and a prophet, said, 'Let your eyes look forward, let your eyelids incline directly; make straight paths with your feet' (Prov. 4:25–26). But the gospel voice gives more rigorous teaching about purity, saying, 'Everyone who sees another's wife to desire her has already committed adultery with her in his heart. And he who marries,' it says, 'a woman divorced by her husband commits adultery, and he who divorces his wife without grounds of fornication makes her commit adultery' (Matt. 5:28, 32). Solomon further says, 'Will anyone put fire in his bosom, and will not burn his clothing? Or will anyone walk on a fire of coals, and will not burn his feet? So he who approaches a married woman will not be guiltless' (Prov. 6:27–29).

And that we not only love our confrères—as some suppose— the prophet Isaiah said, 'Tell those who hate you and curse you, "You are our brothers", so that the name of the Lord may be glorified and may appear in their gladness' (Is. 66:5). And the gospel: 'Love', it says, 'your enemies and pray for those who abuse you. For if you love those who love you, what kind of reward do you have? Brigands and tax collectors too do this' (Matt. 5:44, 46; Luke 6:27, 32). It teaches those who do good not to boast, so that they may not be sycophants. For 'let not', it says, 'your left hand know what your right hand is doing' (Matt. 6:3). And further, concerning 'being subordinate to principalities and powers' (Tit. 3:1) and 'praying for them' the divine Word gives us a command, 'so that we may lead a quiet and peaceable life' (1 Tim. 2:1–2). And it teaches us to render everything [due] to all: 'honor to whom honor is due, respect to whom respect is due, fear to whom fear is due, taxes to whom taxes are due—to owe no one anything except to love all' (Rom. 13:7–8).

It is obvious that Proverbs, Isaiah, the Gospel (of Matthew?), and the Pauline epistles are all expressions of the holy or divine Word. The fact that Theophilus refers to Proverbs

24:21–22 in his first book as from 'the law of God' and in
the second book quotes Genesis from 'the divine scripture'
is related to his apologetic purpose, not to the history of
the New Testament canon. Indeed, he never speaks of
Jesus and the disciples, and he derives the name 'Christian'
from chrism. When an author is obviously concealing much
of his religious tradition we cannot expect him to say much
about its books. It is surprising that we find anything at all.
We have to pay attention to the allusions in order to see
the extent of the New Testament influence on Theophilus'
mind. For example, there are 15 to 1 Corinthians, 11 to
John, 8 apiece to Matthew and Luke, and 7 to Romans.

Finally, it should be clear that early Christian authors do
not always simply reproduce the New Testament writings.
This fact is especially obvious at one point in Theophilus'
work (2, 27). Paul had written that 'as by one man's disobedience many were made sinners, so by one man's obedience many will be made righteous' (Rom. 5:19, RSV).
Theophilus begins as Paul did but develops his own thought
in quite a different direction. 'Just as by disobedience the
man acquired death for himself'—thus far, from Paul—'so
by obeying the will of God, whoever will can obtain eternal
life for himself. For God gave us a law and holy commandments (cf. Rom. 5:12); everyone who performs them can be
saved (cf. Matt. 19:16–19 and parallels) and, attaining to
the resurrection, can inherit imperishability (1 Cor. 15:50).'
Theophilus is using Pauline phrases but is reinterpreting
them by placing them in a non-Pauline context. We may
recall that Ignatius made use of the same procedure.[1]

This is to say that while for Theophilus the Pauline

---

[1] E. Barnikol (*Texte und Untersuchungen* 77, 1961, 102–3) has
argued that the New Testament passages in *Ad Autol.* 3, 13–14 come
from a 'neutestamentliche Überarbeitung', but the evidence supplied
for this revision is inconclusive.

epistles are almost indubitably 'scripture', they are treated in a context which involves other New Testament writings which represent different points of view. Just as Theophilus (like other second-century theologians) is concerned with synthesizing the Old Testament and the contents of the New, so he is concerned with combining Paul's teaching with that of Christ and other apostles.

Before going on to the end of the second century we should summarize what we have found in the works of the apologists. (1) For all of them the synoptic gospels are authoritative. Justin speaks of them as gospels; Athenagoras refers to them as sources of Christian teaching; Theophilus uses the expressions 'gospel voice' and 'gospel'. (2) It is highly probable that both Justin and Athenagoras knew the Gospel of John; Tatian and Theophilus certainly knew it. Theophilus referred to its author as inspired by the Spirit. (3) Other gospels were certainly in circulation, and Tatian seems to be making use of something like the gospels of *Thomas* and *Philip*; apparently, however, he was aware that they were not generally used. (4) As for the Pauline epistles, Justin provides nothing but allusions, probably because of the Marcionite crisis at Rome; his disciple Tatian follows his example in an apologetic work, although elsewhere he provides explicit quotations and exegesis. Athenagoras too alludes to the epistles in his apology, though the treatise *On the Resurrection* contains an explicit reference to 'the apostle'. Theophilus offers many allusions and once speaks of 'the divine Word' as the source—or the content—of Paul's letters. (5) Clear Allusions to Hebrews occur in Tatian, and Theophilus. (6) Tatian's probable rejection of 1–2 Timothy is unique, perhaps Gnostic in origin. Allusions to 1 Timothy occur in Athanagoras, and Theophilus treats 1 Timothy and Titus as Pauline. (7) It is harder to find traces of the non-Pauline letters, although in Theophilus there are allusions to 1 Peter and 1 John. (8) Justin explicitly says that Revelation was written by 'John, one of the disciples of Christ', and allusions to the book appear again in Theophilus.

The authoritative character of these New Testament books is not open to question. The gospels were certainly read at Christian worship in Justin's time, and he mentions them ahead of the Old Testament prophets. Melito of Sardis speaks of the Old Testament as consisting of 'old books', and his statement implies the existence of a collection of 'new books'. Athenagoras refers to the gospels as the source of Christian teaching. Theophilus clearly views the gospels and the epistles as just as authoritative as the prophetic writings.

On the other hand, these authors do not usually call the New Testament books 'scripture'; they do not usually employ the expression 'it is written' in regard to their content. What this means is not quite clear, for in arguing with Jewish or gentile opponents an appeal to New Testament 'scripture' as an authority would not be of much use. From some of the Apostolic Fathers we know that the New Testament books were close to being viewed as 'scripture', and the Gnostic Basilides certainly regarded them in this light. We should assume that, while the Old Testament continued to be the primary 'scripture' of the second-century Church, the New Testament books were in process of being recognized as scriptural.

Several sections of the Sermon on the Mount deserve special attention because their use by second-century writers illustrates how freely the gospels were quoted

Matt. 5:28 (Athenag. 32)		
Everyone who looks at a woman to desire her has already committed adultery with her in his heart.		

Matt. 5:32		
Everyone who divorces his wife without grounds of fornication makes her commit adultery, and whoever marries a divorced woman commits adultery.		

Matt. 5:44–46	Luke 6:27–28	Did. 1:3
I say to you, Love your enemies, Bless those who curse,[1] (Pray for your enemies)[2] and pray for those who persecute you, so that you may become sons of your Father in heaven, for he makes his sun rise upon the evil and the good, and makes it rain upon the just and unjust.[3]	I say to you . . . Love your enemies . . . Do well to those who hate you, Bless those who curse you. Pray for those who abuse you.	Bless those who curse and pray for your ener

	Luke 6:32–34	
For if you love those who love you, what reward have you? Do not tax collectors do the same?	And if you love those who love you, what credit is that to you? Sinners do the same.	For (b) if you love t who love you, (a) credit is it? (c) Do no gentiles do the same? you, love those who you.

1 Inserted from Luke in some manuscripts of Matthew; so Athenag. 11, 1.

2 Added in Oxyrhynchus Papyrus 1224.

3 Athenagoras quotes this exactly, except that he reads 'the Father who i heaven'.

Justin, *Ap.* 1, 15, 1	Theoph. 3, 13
Whoever looks at a woman to desire her has already committed adultery in his heart, in God's view.	Everyone who looks at another's wife to desire her has already committed adultery with her in his heart.

Justin, *Ap.* 1, 15, 3	Theoph. 3, 13
He who marries a woman divorced by her husband commits adultery.	(b) He who divorces his wife without grounds of fornication makes her commit adultery; (a) he who marries a woman divorced by her husband commits adultery.

Justin 1, 15, 9	Theoph. 3, 14
(b) I say to you, Pray for your enemies and love those who hate you and bless those who curse you and pray for those who abuse you.	Love your enemies and pray for those who abuse you.

Clem. 13:4		
If you love those who ℯ you, (a) it is no credit /ou,[4] (c) but it is a credit you love enemies and ℈se who hate you.	(a) If you love those who love you, what new thing do you do? The fornicators too do this.	For if you love those who love you, what reward do you have? Brigands and tax-collectors too do this.

4 See also Ignatius, *Polyc.* 2:1: 'If you love good disciples, it is no credit to you.'

X

The New Testament books
at the end of the second century

During the course of the second century the basic collection
of the New Testament books came to be firmly established
among Christians, Gnostic and 'orthodox' alike. There was
a nucleus of writings which almost all accepted, consisting
of four gospels, an indeterminate number of Pauline epistles
(though usually ten or thirteen), a few other letters (usually
1 Peter and 1 John), and the book of Revelation. The book
of Acts seems to be reflected in 1 Clement and Justin's
Apology but not elsewhere. In addition to these basic books
many Christian writers continued to use books later
declared apocryphal, and oral traditions as well.

The books in the basic collection were sometimes called
'scripture', but a certain hesitation over the use of this term
for anything but the Old Testament seems to have continued.
It is also probable that, except in discussions with Jewish
critics, the question of what was 'scripture' and what was
not did not seem especially important.

Serapion of Antioch

The question of what books to use continued to present
difficulties, at Antioch and elsewhere, until at least the end

of the seond century. About 190 Serapion of Antioch visited Rhossus, a village in his diocese, and found that disagreement had arisen over a gospel ascribed to Peter. He settled the issue rather hastily by giving his permission for the book to be read; he does not say whether publicly or privately. He supposed that all the Christians at Rhossus 'held to the true faith' and therefore would be reading only orthodox books. When he returned to Antioch, however, he was able to obtain a copy from some Docetists (who perhaps supposed that the bishop was ripe for conversion) and then discovered, presumably by comparing it with the accepted apostolic gospels, that it contained some additions to 'the Savior's true teaching'. (We should add that the book cannot have contained the tradition about Peter which Ignatius knew— p. 101f.—for it was being used by Docetists who supposed that Christ merely 'seemed' to have a human body.)

Serapion makes a statement in which the difficulties concerning 'fringe' literature become very clear. He accepts, he says, Peter and the other apostles 'as Christ' (compare Galatians 4:14), but he rejects the writings falsely ascribed to them, since he knows that they were not handed down by tradition.[1] This statement shows that two criteria were involved in acceptance of such books. (1) The books had to be genuinely apostolic; this means that they had to be consonant with the books of the basic collection, universally regarded as apostolic. (2) They had to be handed down by tradition from the apostolic age. Had they been read by early Christians, they would still be read; and if orthodox Christians were now reading them, it could be presupposed that they were early. A book used by the unorthodox might be trustworthy, but it needed to be examined with care. These two criteria obviously led to difficulties, for (1) there are differences between the Gospel of John and the synoptic

1 Eusebius, *H. E.* 6, 12, 3–6.

gospels, as the Alogi (see below) were insisting, and furthermore (2) in various centers Christians were accustomed to read various books (see Chapter XI). Perhaps Serapion was aware of the difficulties, but the tone of his letter suggests that he was not.

It is worth noting that the question of 'scripture' did not arise in the course of this discussion, as far as we know; and nothing Serapion says would indicate that it could have arisen. The question was not, 'Are these books to be counted as "scripture"?' but 'Are these books apostolic and orthodox?'[1]

The Alogi and Gaius of Rome

The questions not solved by Serapion were being raised by the Alogi, apparently in Asia Minor in the second century, and by the Roman presbyter Gaius early in the third. The Alogi, whose nickname was given them because they rejected the Gospel of John with its teaching about the Logos ('alogos' also means 'irrational'), were apparently troubled by the use which adherents of the 'new prophecy' were making of the Gospel and the Book of Revelation. The Montanists spoke of their teacher as the new Paraclete (John 14:26, etc.) and expected the imminent descent of the new Jerusalem (Rev. 21:2). The Alogi responded by ascribing both books to the Jewish-Christian heretic Cerinthus, by comparing the Gospel with the synoptics to show that it did not agree with them, and by ridiculing the apocalyptic imagery of Revelation. Gaius, in his *Dialogue* with the Montanist Proclus, took the same line, contrasting

---

1 Serapion's difficulties *may* have been increased if his predecessor Theophilus used the *Teaching of Peter*; cf. E. v. Dobschütz, *Das Kerygma Petri* (Leipzig, 1893), 57.

details in Revelation with passages from the Gospel of Matthew, the Pauline epistles, and parts of the Old Testament. In addition, Gaius accepted only thirteen Pauline epistles, like Irenaeus (see p. 154) rejecting Hebrews.[1] Presumably he used similar comparisons between Hebrews and the Pauline letters to support his case.

The work of the Alogi and Gaius in regard to the Johannine books does not necessarily imply that there was widespread doubt about their authoritative character. On the contrary, it seems to reflect a deliberate effort to take away the authority ascribed to them by the Montanists as by other Christians. Presumably Epiphanius, writing about A.D. 375, did not quote their exact words, but he correctly represented their general position. 'They say that since the Gospel according to John does not say the same things [as do the synoptic gospels] it is uncanonical (*adiatheton*) and they will not accept it.'[2] We cannot press the late word *adiatheton*, but it suggests that the Alogi knew of a collection generally accepted—and were proposing a different one. Other Christians viewed their proposal without enthusiasm.

Irenaeus of Lyons

Probably the most important statements about the New Testament in the late second century are those provided by Irenaeus, missionary bishop of Lyons, who wrote five books against heresies about 185. His statements are important because they are much more extensive than anything we have encountered before. They are also important because Irenaeus was closely associated in his youth with Polycarp of Smyrna and later came into close contact with the traditional

1 Eusebius, *H. E.* 6, 20, 3.
2 *Pan.* 51, 18.

views of the Roman church. Although we cannot exclude the possibility that sometimes he speaks for himself, he is ordinarily concerned with maintaining and transmitting a tradition which he regards as essentially uniform. If there is anything novel about his views of the New Testament books, we may suppose that it lies in the way he expresses them, not in the views themselves. He is almost certainly a reliable witness to the situation not only in Gaul in his time but also to that in Rome and Asia Minor during the generation before him.

We have already discussed his use of the Old Testament, which consisted of the books in the commonly accepted Greek version and included the additions to Daniel, Baruch, 2 Esdras, and 1 Enoch. Sometimes, as A. Benoit has shown, he made use of collections of texts;[1] more often he turned to the Old Testament itself. It would appear that when he thought of the New Testament in relation to the Old he sometimes had two similar collections of books in mind; one consisted of 'the law and the prophets', the other of 'evangelical and apostolical' documents.[2] The titles of the second collection may, of course, have been suggested to him by Marcion; but we should assume that in this regard Marcion was reflecting Christian usage, not vice versa.

Irenaeus definitely had a New Testament, even though he did not give it this title, and he regarded its contents as 'scripture', even though this conception of it was not crucial in his thought. Ordinarily, like the Valentinian Gnostics against whom he was chiefly arguing, he differentiated (1) the Old Testament scriptures, (2) the teaching of the Lord, and (3) the teaching of the apostles and their followers. Only

---

1 *Texte und Untersuchungen* 79 (1961), 20–27.
2 *Adv. haer.* 1, 3, 6; F. Vernet in *Dictionnaire de theologie catholique* VII (Paris, 1923), 2417.

once, indeed, did he refer to a verse from a Pauline epistle (Gal. 5:21) as from 'the scriptures'[1]—although he was deeply concerned with proving that it was one and the same Spirit which inspired the prophets, the apostles, and the elders of the apostolic Church (see Acts 15:28). Because the work of the Spirit continued to be expressed in later writings, he could refer to a passage from the *Shepherd* of Hermas as from 'scripture'.[2] In addition, he provided three quotations from sayings of Jesus not found in the gospels and ascribed to them an authority no different from that of the gospels themselves.[3]

Irenaeus was the first Christian writer to provide an explicit statement about the gospels universally recognized. He stated that there were four, and only four; those written by Matthew, Mark, Luke, and John. Matthew and John were apostles; Mark and Luke were disciples of Peter and Paul. Irenaeus' gospel collection, like that to which Justin earlier alluded, was thus entirely apostolic in origin, and the rest of his New Testament (so to speak) consisted of books written by three of the four apostles already mentioned. It is well known that he insisted upon the quaternity of the gospels (analogous to the four winds, four corners of the earth, etc.); it now appears that he also had four principal apostles to write, and be responsible for, his collection of New Testament books. Luke, Paul's disciple, wrote Acts, as Irenaeus proves by using the methods of literary criticism;[4] Paul wrote a number of epistles (apparently thirteen); and John, the Lord's disciple, wrote not only a gospel but also the book of Revelation and either one or two letters. In tabular form Irenaeus' list of apostolic witnesses is as follows:

1 *Adv. haer.* 1, 6, 3.
2 *Ibid.*, 4, 20, 2.
3 *Ibid.*, 2, 46, 1; 5, 36, 1; *Epideixis* 43 (ed. J. P. Smith, p. 182 n. 207).
4 See *The Earliest Lives of Jesus* (London–New York, 1961), 32.

Matthew	Peter	Paul	John
Gospel	1 Peter	Epistles	Gospel
	Sermons in Acts	Acts	Revelation
	Gospel of Mark	Gospel of Luke	Epistle(s)

We have suggested that he knew thirteen Pauline epistles. There seems to be an allusion to Hebrews 1:3 at one point in his volumes, and this allusion, without any reference to Paul, is the only one;[1] according to Stephanus Gobarus (sixth century), Irenaeus rejected the Pauline authorship of Hebrews.[2] Eusebius' statement that he used 'testimonies' from Hebrews and from the Wisdom of Solomon tells us nothing about how he viewed the authorship or canonicity of either book.[3] He explicitly referred, however, to the titles or the Pauline authorship of twelve epistles, including the Pastorals but not Philemon (which he probably had no occasion to use). In order of frequency, his quotations and allusions run thus: 1 Corinthians (102), Romans (84), Ephesians (37), Galatians (27), 2 Corinthians (18), Colossians (18), Philippians (13), 2 Thessalonians (9), 1 Timothy (5), 2 Timothy (5), Titus (4), and 1 Thessalonians (2).

We have already seen (Chapter VIII) that the Valentinian Gnostic Ptolemaeus could speak of what 'Paul said in 1 Corinthians'. This kind of explicit reference appears again in Irenaeus' writings, where we encounter mention of Paul's letters to the Romans, the Galatians, the Ephesians, the Philippians, and the Colossians. There is also a reference to the epistles (plural) to Timothy and a quotation from Titus with the formula 'as Paul says'.[4] In citations from the

1 *Adv. haer.* 2, 30, 9.
2 Migne, PG 103, 1104D.
3 *H. E.* 5, 26.
4 *Adv. haer.* 3, 3, 3–4.

epistles to the Corinthians and the Thessalonians there is a slight trace of confusion; usually the letters are differentiated as 'first' and 'second', but once I Corinthians is called 'that epistle which is to the Corinthians'[1] and once 2 Thessalonians is 'that epistle which is to the Thessalonians'.[2] This kind of citation recalls Clement's naming I Corinthians 'the epistle of Paul the apostle' (I Clem. 47:1), but Irenaeus is likely simply to be quoting from memory.

When Irenaeus refers to what Peter said, he is usually quoting from Peter's sermons in the books of Acts; but once, when he speaks of 'what was said by Peter', he is referring to I Peter.[3] (There are no traces of 2 Peter or of Jude in Irenaeus' writings.)

As for the Johannine epistles, Irenaeus cites I John in *Adversus haereses* 3, 16, 5 and, three paragraphs later, refers back to the same epistle but quotes from 2 John. He may have regarded 1-2 John as one letter; perhaps he was quoting from memory. One should remember, however, how difficult it was in antiquity to be sure that references were correct. It was (and is) quite possible to read a Greek manuscript in which there are no word divisions; but to differentiate works rather similar in content was not easy. Irenaeus also knew and prized the book of Revelation, written by John, the Lord's disciple, author of the Gospel.[4]

In his writings there are only two possible allusions to James,[5] and presumably he did not regard it as a theological authority, universally accepted, if he knew it at all.

Irenaeus thus had a 'New Testament' of about twenty-two books. The total will vary depending on whether or not we include Philemon (as we probably should), regard 2 John

1 *Ibid.*, 3, 11, 9.
2 *Ibid.*, 4, 27, 4.
3 *Ibid.*, 5, 7, 2.
4 *Ibid.*, 5, 30, 2.
5 *Ibid.*, 4, 16, 2 (James 2:23); 5, 1, 1 (James 1:18; 22).

as separate from 1 John (uncertain), and include Hermas (unlikely?). Since Irenaeus was so thoroughly convinced of the mystical importance of numbers, we may wonder whether or not he had a 'basic' collection comparable to his 'basic' Old Testament, in which there were also about twenty-two books. But in view of the possible variations existing in both collections we cannot make any definite statement.

Much more important than the number or the order—about which we know only that the gospels had the sequence current today—is the fact that Irenaeus indubitably had a clearly defined collection of apostolic books. He regarded them as more important than the Old Testament, since he viewed the Old Testament revelation as merely preparatory to that given by Christ to his apostles, and interpreted the former in relation to the latter. He was not especially concerned with the 'scriptural' status of these books, though he did regard them as 'scripture'.

The Muratorian Fragment

From the end of the second century comes an interesting and important fragment called Muratorian because it was published by L. A. Muratori in 1740. The date is known because the author said that the *Shepherd* of Hermas could not be read in church since it was written (1) recently and (2) when Pius was bishop of Rome (142–55). A mention of Rome simply as 'the city' suggests that the document comes from the Roman church.

Something is missing at the beginning, but it must have dealt with the first of the four gospels recognized by the author, since he provides information about Mark, Luke, and John (in that order). His statements about the evangelists contain answers to criticisms largely based on the differences among them; he is thus replying to Marcionites (by setting Luke in the context of four books) and to critics like the Alogi (by insisting on the importance of John). He also says that 'the acts of all the apostles are written in one book' by Luke, a witness to these acts; these statements are directed against admirers of the apocryphal books of Acts. His list of Pauline epistles has made a good deal of trouble for scholars, since it seems to be so different from other lists. First he starts with Corinthians, then continues with Galatians, and ends with Romans. Then he says that he does not need to discuss the individual epistles, 'since the blessed Paul himself, following the order of his predecessor John, writes only to seven churches by name, in the following order: (1) to the Corinthians, (2) to the Ephesians, (3) to the Philippians, (4) to the Colossians, (5) to the Galatians, (6) to the Thessalonians, and (7) to the Romans'. What kind of order is this?

In order to show the measure of variation in the Muratorian epistle-list from those found elsewhere we compare its sequence with three others.

Marcion	*Muratorian*	*'ordinary'*	*Beatty papyri*
Galatians		Romans	Romans + Hebrews
1–2 Corinthians	1–2 Corinthians	1–2 Corinthians	1–2 Corinthians
Romans		Galatians	
1–2 Thessalonians			
Laodiceans (=Eph.)	Ephesians	Ephesians	Ephesians
			Galatians
	Philippians	Philippians	Philippians
Colossians	Colossians	Colossians	Colossians

Marcion	*Muratorian*	*'ordinary'*	*Beatty papyri*
Philippians	Galatians		
	1–2	1–2	1 (–2)
	Thessalonians	Thessalonians	Thessalonians
	Romans		

This table suggests that the basic conclusion of N. A. Dahl is right: that the author of the Muratorian list, writing primarily against Marcion, reflects the norm found in the 'ordinary' sequence but has transferred Marcion's favorites to the end, perhaps in part because he is aiming at a chronological order.[1] The 'ordinary' sequence is also reflected in the Beatty papyri of the early third century, where the placing of Hebrews after Romans suggests that there was some doubt as to where to put it. Perhaps there was also some doubt about the location of the letter to the Galatians.

The fragment goes on to speak of personal letters which have universal significance: these consist of Philemon, Titus, and 1–2 Timothy. The author also accepts Jude, 1–2 John, the Wisdom of Solomon (though, he says, it was not written by Solomon himself), and the Revelations of John and of Peter (though some will not permit the latter to be read in church). The *Shepherd* of Hermas, he emphatically states, is neither prophetic nor apostolic, and therefore cannot be publicly read.

Beyond such books as these lie the forgeries of the Marcionites—the epistles to the Laodiceans and the Alexandrians and a book of Marcionite psalms—and the writings of Valentinus and Basilides, not to mention (and the mention is quite garbled in its present form) the treatises of the Montanists. The author may not have known much about the books he rejected, for the Marcionites' Laodiceans was the Church's Ephesians. Conceivably, the 'letter to the Alexandrians' was what we know as Hebrews.

1 *Zeitschrift für die neutestamentliche Wissenschaft* 52 (1961), 39–53.

In many respects the basic list of the Muratorian fragment is identical with what we have found in Irenaeus' writings. The Muratorian omission of 1 Peter is striking, even shocking; and it is very likely that, as Zahn held, a mention of this letter has fallen out. As for the Muratorian criticism of Hermas, we do not know whether or not Irenaeus would have considered the *Shepherd* as a book to be read in church. We may suggest, however, that he would not have had it publicly read, especially in view of its length.

This leaves us with two novelties in the Muratorian list. First, Jude has come to be accepted, presumably because of its militant advocacy of tradition and denunciation of heretics. If the list included 1 Peter as well as Jude, its content was identical with what we find in Clement and Tertullian, about the same time. Second, the Wisdom of Solomon is somehow included in the New Testament list. This cannot be right, unless the 'friends of Solomon' to whom the author ascribes it were Christians. Perhaps they were; perhaps he was aware that by Jews the book was almost universally rejected, while Christians were making increasing use of it.

A Bodmer Papyrus

Finally, we should say something about one of the volumes of the Bodmer papyri. In its original form, early in the third century, it contained the apocryphal 'infancy gospel' of James, the apocryphal letters of Paul from and to the Corinthians (3 Corinthians), 'Ode of Solomon' (the 11th), the Epistle of Jude, the paschal sermon by Melito of Sardis, a fragment of a hymn, and 1–2 Peter. This collection is very strange. If one were to allow for the possibility of 'guilt by association', one would infer that Jude and 1–2 Peter were regarded as edifying but not canonical. On the other hand, the compiler of the papyrus book may well have been draw-ing his materials from various kinds of collections—we do not know what principle he followed—and, since Origen, very little later, like the copyist of the papyrus in Egypt, referred to Jude and 1 Peter and alluded to 2 Peter,[1] we should not deny that there these books were included in the canon.

From what we have seen, then, we should state that by this time the main outlines of the New Testament were perfectly clear and almost universally accepted. There were four gospels together with the book of Acts; there were usually thirteen Pauline epistles; there was also an epistle (rarely two) by Peter, one or two by John, one by Jude; and there was a Revelation by John. The status of Hebrews and 3 John (unless included with 1–2 John) remained doubtful. There is no definite proof that anyone outside Egypt (see Chapter XI) regarded James and 2 Peter as canonical, although their later acceptance suggests that some churches did so regard them.

The Anonymous against Montanism

We must admit, however, that the expression 'New Testa-ment' was rarely used in relation to a collection of books. The passages where Irenaeus uses it are all fairly ambiguous and may refer only to the new 'covenant'. As we have already said, Melito's 'books of the old covenant' do not necessarily imply the existence of a New Testament. As W. C. van Unnik has written, 'the first unequivocal connection be-tween *hē kainē diathēkē* and Christian literature is found in a refutation of Montanism by an anonymous author,

1 Jude: *Princ.* 3, 2, 1; 'Peter in his first epistle': *Princ.* 2, 5, 3.

writing in 192/193'.[1] This author (quoted by Eusebius, *H. E.* 5, 16, 3) says that he had hesitated to write an anti-Montanist treatise 'from fear and extreme caution, lest perchance I might seem to some to be adding a new article or clause to the word of the new covenant (*kainē diathēkē*) of the gospel, to which no one who has intended to live in accordance with the gospel itself may add, from which no one may take away'. It is evident that he is speaking about a relatively closed collection of books, but that his own treatise might conceivably be included in it. It is also evident that he does not explicitly refer to the collection as 'the New Testament'. Indeed, even in Origen's earlier period (shortly before 231) the expression still seemed rather strange. He speaks of 'what is called' the Old Testament and the 'so styled' New Testament.[2]

We must therefore recognize that at the end of the second century, although the New Testament books were regarded as authoritative, apostolic, and indeed inspired, they were not called 'the New Testament'.

---

1 *Texte und Untersuchungen* 79 (1961), 217.
2 Origen, *Ioh. comm.* 5, 8, quoted by Van Unnik, *op. cit.*, 214 n. 1.

F

XI

Alexandria and the New Testament

It is difficult to exaggerate the importance of the Christian community at Alexandria in relation to the Church's concern for literary and theological questions—in short, for its coming to terms with Graeco-Roman culture. Unfortunately, what we know about the early history of the Church there is by no means comparable to the significance of the historical process. Certainly the Jewish philospher Philo, who later strongly influenced Christian thought, lived and wrote there. Possibly the Epistle to the Hebrews and the Epistle of Barnabas are Alexandrian in origin. The Gnostic Basilides certainly taught at Alexandria. But of 'orthodox' Christianity at Alexandria we know very little until the end of the second century, when Clement tells us something about his teacher Pantaenus. What he tells us is that Pantaenus was able to explain why Hebrews did not bear Paul's name; this was because Paul was an apostle to the gentiles and therefore did not wish to write the Hebrews as if he were their apostle.[1] This statement shows that literary questions were being asked at Alexandria; it also shows that Hebrews had been accepted there, at least by Pantaenus and his circle.

Before we turn to Clement, however, we should recall our claim that Basilides represents the ideas about the New

1 Eusebius, *H. E.* 6, 14.

Testament books which presumably were current, at least in limited groups, at Alexandria two generations before Clement's time. New Testament books were regarded, then and there, as scripture. We need not expect Clement to reveal innovations in this respect. All we can look for is greater precision in a choice of books, especially in relation to the apocryphal writings produced by Gnostics or semi-Gnostics during the second-century.

Another point which we must bear in mind as we look at the works of the most important Alexandrian theologians, Clement and Origen, is that they actually do reflect such increasing precision and that the degree to which it is absent or present depends, in part, on the circumstances in which the works were written. We shall see, for example, that Clement's views about the gospels became considerably clearer at a definite point in his *Stromata*, and that Origen's ideas were somewhat different, when expressed at Caesarea, from what they were when he was at Alexandria. In addition, we must remember that both writers were influenced by the views of other Christians, not only those at Alexandria or, in Origen's case, at Caesarea but also those who came to Alexandria or were visited by Alexandrians. Generally speaking, Clement and Origen reflect Alexandrian usage; but at some points they may reflect views held elsewhere.

Finally, since Clement was the master of a private school of Christian apologetics and of what he called 'Gnosis', we cannot expect that his views of the canon will be as fully representative of the Church's teaching as will those of Origen, the real founder of the catechetical school at Alexandria under the bishop's direction. Where Clement wavers, Origen is usually firm. This difference is largely due to the difference between individual opinion and semi-official Church doctrine. Clement's teaching at Alexandria came to an end during the persecution under Septimius Severus

F*

(A.D. 202), when he left the city, never to return. At this point the bishop Demetrius invited the young Origen to direct a school under Church auspices, and he was its head until, in conflict with Demetrius' successor, he too left Alexandria, in 231. Dionysius, head of the school after Origen, became bishop of Alexandria in 247.

We can understand the problem of the New Testament canon at Alexandria only in relation to the history of these schools and of their rivals, Hellenistic Jewish and Gnostic. Especially in the writings of Clement there is a certain vagueness about the distinction between writings generally regarded as canonical and those which were never, or hardly ever, accepted elsewhere. This point holds good for the Old Testament as well as for the New. Clement's Greek Bible included not only the books generally accepted by Jews but, in addition, such writings as Baruch, Sirach, the Wisdom of Solomon, Tobit, Judith, and 1–2 Maccabees. He knew the Greek additions to Esther and Daniel, including the story of Susanna.[1] His Old Testament authorities were not confined to this list, however, for in his works we encounter 1 Enoch (which he says was written before the Psalms)[2] and 2 Esdras.[3] Conceivably he was introduced to these books by the Epistle of Barnabas, which he valued very highly, and to the *Assumption of Moses* by the Epistle of Jude (for he quotes from the *Assumption* when giving exegesis of Jude).[4] It is more likely, however, that he simply knew a large collection of Jewish apocalyptic works not unlike the collection which Barnabas knew, for in addition he provides a fairly extensive quotation from an *Apocalypse of Zephaniah*.[5]

1 Full discussion by J. Ruwet in *Biblica* 29 (1948), 93–94.
2 *Eclogae propheticae* 53, 4; not in *Stromata*.
3 *Str.* 3, 100, 4.
4 *Adumbr. Jud.*; *Str.* 1, 153–54; 6, 132, 2–3.
5 *Str.* 5, 77, 2.

On the fringe of the New Testament, and beyond it, there were many documents which later, and probably by most Christians outside Alexandria, were not regarded as authoritative. Among these were gospels *According to the Hebrews* and *According to the Egyptians*, not to mention such an esoteric treatise as the *Traditions of Matthias*.[1] Clement's ideas about the status of such documents do not seem to have been altogether clear. It is plain enough that his own New Testament contained gospels, for in his earlier writings he refers to those according to Matthew, Luke, and John. But in Books 2 and 3 of his *Stromata* his ideas about canonical authority are a little vague; they get clearer as he continues to write. In *Stromata* 2, 45, 5 he introduces a quotation with the words, 'It is written in the *Gospel according to the Hebrews*'. In *Stromata* 3, 45, 3 he takes over a quotation from the *Gospel according to the Egyptians* without naming the book. A little farther on (3, 63–66) he quotes from what he 'thinks' is *Egyptians*; in other words, he has not checked his references. By the time he writes *Stromata* 3, 92–93 he is finally sure that the quotation does come from *Egyptians*; and here he stops to point out that the Church accepts four gospels and four only; *Egyptians* is not one of them. When he quotes from the *Gospel according to the Hebrews* in *Stromata* 5, 96, 3—and does not say what his source is—he may be reverting to his older, more 'permissive' attitude, or he may be realizing that he should not name the book.[2]

Clement clearly recognized the book of Acts as scripture, and he accepted all the Pauline epistles including Hebrews. His own theory about Hebrews was different from that of Pantaenus; he held that Paul wrote in Hebrew and that Luke

1 Ruwet, *op. cit.*, 401–2; *Matthias* in *Str.* 2, 45, 5; 7, 82, 1.
2 *Ibid.*, 396–98.

translated his epistle into Greek. The theory is untenable but, like most such theories, ingenious.[1]

In addition, he acknowledged the Johannine authorship of the Apocalypse[2] and definitely accepted 1 Peter, 1–2 John, and Jude as part of the New Testament. Also, he regarded the *Didache* as scripture[3] and viewed 1 Clement, Barnabas, Hermas, and the *Preaching* and *Revelation of Peter* as inspired. These books were either canonical or close to being canonical.[4]

In quoting from the gospels, Clement ordinarily relies on them not as books but as sources for the teaching of Jesus; explicit references to particular books are rather unusual. (In this respect Clement is closer to Irenaeus than to Origen.) He does speak once of 'the Gospel according to Matthew', and in a homily refers to Matthew's having added several phrases to the Beatitudes.[5] In the same homily he calls the second gospel 'according to Mark',[6] and in fragments of his lost *Hypotyposes* he describes Mark's work as an evangelist at Rome.[7] A letter discovered by Morton Smith reveals that he knew several versions of Mark: the one generally used, the forgery employed by Carpocratian Gnostics, and a secret book which Mark wrote at Alexandria. The third gospel was written by Luke, who also composed the Acts of the Apostles.[8] John wrote the last, 'spiritual' gospel, as well as 'the major epistle' (hence also a minor one—'to virgins') and the book of Revelation.[9]

Clement has a collection of fourteen Pauline epistles (including Hebrews). He explicitly mentions all of them

1 Eusebius, *H. E.* 6, 14; for Acts, *Str.* 6, 63, 5.
2 *Paed.* 2, 108, 3; *Str.* 6, 106, 2.
3 *Str.* 1, 100, 4.
4 Ruwet, *op. cit.*, 391–96; 402–3.
5 *Str.* 1, 47, 5; *Quis div. salv.* 17, 5.
6 *Quis div. salv.* 5, 1.
7 Stählin III 197–98, 206.
8 *Paed.* 2, 15, 2; *Str.* 1, 145, 2.
9 Stählin III 197, 215; *Str.* 6, 106, 2.

except Philemon, and we must assume that like Irenaeus he passes over Philemon because he has no occasion to mention it. He gives references to Romans, Galatians, Ephesians, Philippians, Colossians, Titus, and Hebrews. When he mentions the Corinthian letters he sometimes differentiates them[1] but more often does not; once he speaks of 1 Corinthians as the letter to the Corinthians.[2] Though he does not name either Thessalonian epistle, he quotes from both. And he differentiates 2 Timothy from 1 Timothy, though while referring to the second letter he actually quotes from the first.[3]

In addition, Clement clearly quotes from 1 Peter ('the epistle'[4]) as well as from the Epistle of Jude;[5] but although Eusebius says that he commented on all the general epistles in his *Hypotyposes*,[6] it is most unlikely that he discussed either James or 2 Peter, of which there are no traces in his major works. We cannot tell whether or not he knew 3 John.

Clement's use of non-canonical New Testament materials presents us with a mixture of continuity and change. Throughout the *Stromata* he makes use of 1 Clement, Barnabas, and Hermas; but he employs the *Didache* only in *Stromata* 1, 100, 4—and there he does not name the work. The *Preaching of Peter* occurs in the first two books of the *Stromata*, but not again until the sixth. Perhaps during the interval Clement was uncertain whether or not to use it. Similarly, the *Traditions of Matthias*, used by Nicolaitan Gnostics according to *Stromata* 3, 26, 3, are quoted in *Stromata* 2 and 7, but not in the interval.[7]

---

1 *Paed.* 1, 33, 1; *Str.* 2, 136, 5; 4, 100, 1.
2 *Str.* 5, 80, 4.
3 *Str.* 3, 53, 4 (1 Tim. 5:9–10).
4 *Str.* 3, 110, 1; 4, 129, 2.
5 *Paed.* 3, 44, 4; *Str.* 3, 11, 2.
6 *H. E.* 6, 14, 1.
7 The *Apocalypse of Peter*, like 1 Enoch, is found only in the *Eclogae propheticae*.

Similarly, while the Gnostic Apelles had quoted 'Become approved money-changers' as 'in the gospel',[1] and Clement himself cites the saying as from scripture in *Stromata* 1, 177, 2, thereafter—presumably because his ideas about scripture are getting clearer—he never quotes it, although he does allude to it. On the other hand, it is in *Stromata* 5, 63, 7 that Clement can write these words: 'in some gospel it says, "Without grudging, the Lord commanded, My mystery is for me and for the sons of my house"'. The use of the expression 'some gospel' at this point is unique; conceivably Clement had in mind the secret Alexandrian Gospel of Mark mentioned in the fragment which Morton Smith discovered, but we do not know that this was so. Given the fact which he had acknowledged, that there are four and only four gospels, he should not have provided this quotation.

In fact, generally speaking Clement does not become more cautious in his use of unwritten sayings ascribed by himself or by others to Jesus. Four quotations occur in the first two books of the *Stromata*; these are as follows. (1) 'You have seen your brother; you have seen your God' (*Str.* 1, 94, 5; quoted again in 2, 70, 5, with the addition of 'Know thyself'[2]). (2) 'Ask for the great things and the small ones will be added for you' (*Str.* 1, 158, 2). (3) The words about money-changers, already mentioned. But immediarely after stating that there are only four gospels Clement proceeds to quote phrases derived from 1 Corinthians 7 and ascribes them to the Lord (*Str.* 3, 97). In the remaining books there are two quotations from such sayings along with four allusions. It would appear that in spite of his statement about the four gospels 'transmitted to us' Clement does not

1 Epiphanius, *Haer.* 44, 2, 6.
2 Compare the Gnostic 'know yourselves' in the *Gospel of Thomas*, Saying 2.

hesitate to make use of other traditions or transmissions. We shall see that Origen does the same thing.

One might ask why early Christian writers like Clement felt free to use unwritten traditions so frequently. Apparently there are several factors in the answer. (1) Christians, like their Gnostic competitors, lived in an environment that was not totally bookish. Such traditions were in circulation and they inevitably used them. (2) Within the New Testament itself (see Chapter III) there was considerable precedent for the use of traditional sayings. Paul referred to them at least in 1 Thessalonians and 1 Corinthians, as well as in the sermon ascribed to him in Acts 20:18–35. (3) Theological authority was still provided not so much by a New Testament as by a gospel reflected in the New Testament books.

In the writings of Clement it is possible to detect traces of increasing, though inconsistent, conservatism in regard to the New Testament books. Much the same situation is to be found in the writings of Origen, partly because of his move from Alexandria to Caesarea, where he undoubtedly found that different books were accepted and rejected. In general, however, he favored inclusiveness, as we can see from his letter to Africanus. Africanus was a polymath who had come to question the authenticity of several Old Testament books because they were not accepted by Jews. Origen's reply made clear the view that whatever was in the Septuagint should be used by Christians, and he therefore made use of the Greek Daniel (with Bel and the Dragon and Susanna), not to mention 1 and 3 Baruch, Judith, 1–2 Maccabees, Tobit, the Wisdom of Sirach, and the Wisdom of Solomon. In addition, he knew the *Assumption of Moses*, the *Apocalypse of Elijah*, the *Ascension of Isaiah*, a book of Iannes and Iambres, a *Prayer of Joseph*, and some of the *Testaments of the Twelve Patriarchs*. Apparently he drew the line at works containing strongly eschatological apocalyptic materials. Thus, unlike Clement, he never used 2 Esdras and while at first he accepted 1 Enoch (*Princ.* 1, 3, 3; 4, 4, 8) he later questioned its authority (*Ioh. comm.* 6, 42; *Num. hom.* 8, 2). Perhaps he also became aware that it was favored by Gnostics.

As for the New Testament, he explicitly rejected the apocryphal gospels of *Thomas, Matthias,* and the *Twelve,* along with that according to the *Egyptians* (*Luc. hom.* 1). Early in his career he relied on the *Acts of Paul,* though not as scripture, but later he rejected the book. We do not know why he did so; perhaps he had become acquainted with the opinion (expressed by Tertullian in his work *De baptismo* 17) that it had been forged by an admirer of Paul. In his view there were four gospels and one book of Acts.[1]

It is significant that, like Clement, Origen makes use of unwritten sayings of Jesus, such as the one about 'asking for great things' (*De oratione* 2, 2; *Sel. in Pss.* 4, 2), that about money-changers (*Ioh. comm.* 19, 2 calls it a 'command of Jesus'; *Matt. comm.* 17, 31 refers to it as 'according to the scripture'). It is also significant that, as we should expect, he uses them much less frequently than Clement did. We may also note that in his list of condemned gospels (*Luc. hom.* 1) he does not include the *Gospel according to the Hebrews,* though he is well aware that it lacks ecclesiastical authorization and authority (*Jer. hom.* 15, 4; *Ioh. comm.* 2, 12; *Matt. comm.* 15, 14). It is not so definitely unorthodox —and by allegorizing it he tries to make it orthodox—as *Egyptians* or *Thomas* or the *Gospel of the Twelve.*

Origen has no clear principle on the basis of which he can definitely reject apocryphal traditions or writings. Indeed, he claims that Paul used the *Apocalypse of Elijah* in 1 Corinthians 2:9[2] and that Ignatius of Antioch relied on

1 On the whole question see J. Ruwet in *Biblica* 23 (1942), 18–42.
2 *Ibid.,* 30 (1949), 517–19.

a 'Teaching of Peter' in Smyrnaeans 3:2 (*Princ.* 1, praef. 8). Apostolic and ecclesiastical tradition thus favored the use of a wide variety of books.

Origen's method of citing the New Testament books is much like Clement's. This is to say that he is continuing the tradition, already in evidence in the works of Irenaeus, according to which the New Testament books were clearly differentiated and could be used as literary authorities. He refers to the four gospels by their authors' names and explicitly mentions all fourteen of the Pauline epistles although in his *Commentary on John* he sometimes refers to 1 Corinthians and 1 Thessalonians simply as Corinthians and Thessalonians. Unlike his predecessors, probably because he wrote so much more than they did, he definitely mentions Paul's letter to Philemon.[1]

It would appear that at first Origen was content to speak of Paul as the author of Hebrews but that, later on, he considered the literary problems involved and reached the conclusion that, though it contains Paul's ideas, it was written by someone else, perhaps Luke or Clement of Rome, both of whom were disciples of the apostles. Ruwet has suggested that his doubts about it arose because he knew that it was not accepted at Rome,[2] but this hypothesis is hard to demonstrate. It is just as likely that he knew about previous discussions of the epistle at Alexandria.

As for the general epistles, he expressed doubts about James, 2–3 John, Jude, and 2 Peter, though the form of his expressions suggests that he was not really worried about either James or Jude.[3] It would appear that while he was at Alexandria he regarded the *Didache*, Hermas and Barnabas as canonical but that after removing to Caesarea he became

1 *Jer. hom.* 20, 2; *Matt. comm. ser.* 66; 72.
2 *Biblica* 23 (1942), 24–26.
3 *Ibid.*, 29–32.

aware that they were not accepted there.[1] His use of 1 Clement does not show whether he regarded it as canonical or not, though if he was willing to admit that Clement might have written Hebrews he obviously could have accepted Clement's own letter. He expressed doubts about the *Kerygma Petri* of which Clement of Alexandria was so fond (*Ioh. comm.* 13, 17).

The books which Origen regarded as authoritative were therefore those written by apostles (Matthew, John, Paul, [1] Peter, [1] John, Revelation, James, and Jude) and disciples of apostles (Mark, Luke [–Acts], Hermas, Barnabas, and perhaps Clement). Other books lacked early and continuous attestation, were probably not written by apostles or their disciples, and perhaps were not easily reconcilable with accepted writings (*Gospel of the Hebrews*—Matthew; 2–3 John—1 John; 2 Peter—1 Peter). At Caesarea he encountered, and shared, an attitude more conservative than that at Alexandria in his earlier years. Though he did not set forth a fully systematic scheme for classifying the books, it would appear that he worked with three basic categories: (1) books universally accepted; (2) books questioned; and (3) books definitely rejected.

Both Clement and Origen freely refer to the New Testament books, and to the other semi-canonical books they employ, as 'scripture'. In an Alexandrian environment this usage is to be expected; we recall that Basilides taught at Alexandria (Chapter VIII). It may be that the usage is not to be explained simply on the basis of geography, however, for both Clement and Origen were allegorizers. This is to say that they believed there were meanings latent in the New Testament texts and that these meanings were due to the work of the Holy Spirit, inspirer of the New Testament authors. Gnostic exegetes had already argued that in the

1 *Ibid.*, 33–38.

sayings of Jesus and the words of the apostles there were hidden meanings which they alone knew. More orthodox exegetes had insisted that the Old Testament writings could be understood correctly only by Christians. What Clement and Origen do is to treat the New Testament writings as the Gnostics had treated the words of Jesus and the apostles and as their predecessors had treated the Old Testament. By calling the New Testament writings 'scripture' they imply that in them are spiritual meanings available only to exegetes also inspired by the Spirit.[1]

The process of defining the New Testament cannot be traced with much accuracy between the death of Origen in 253 and the time early in the fourth century when Eusebius of Caesarea wrote his *Church History*. It is evident, however, that the sifting which Origen reflects continued during the next generation. Indeed, a famous treatise by Dionysius of Alexandria *On Promises* contains an analysis of the language, style, and thought of the Gospel and (first) Epistle of John, on the one hand, and Revelation, on the other. Dionysius intends to show that two authors were involved. Since, according to tradition, an apostle wrote the Gospel and the Epistle and another John wrote Revelation, obviously the latter work was written by a disciple of the apostles and therefore did not possess quite the same degree of authority as the other books. Dionysius thus reflects the effort to delineate a canon within the New Testament canon; he plays Gospel against Revelation at the latter's expense—in order to diminish the apocalyptic fervor of Egyptian monks in his diocese.

Much of our information about the views of the Alexandrians on the canon comes to us from Eusebius. He is their heir, as he is the heir of Origen's library at Caesarea. It is therefore no surprise when we find his New Testament

1 On this point see *The Letter and the Spirit* (London, 1957).

to be essentially Alexandrian in content. In the *Church History* (3, 25) he presents a rather confusing classification of New Testament books. It is clearer—naturally enough— in regard to what is 'acknowledged' and what is definitely heretical than in regard to what lies between these categories. What is universally acknowledged consists of the four gospels, the Pauline epistles (he does not say how many), 1 John, 1 Peter, and *perhaps* the Revelation of John. What is absolutely rejected includes the apocryphal gospels ascribed to Peter, Thomas, Matthias, and others, and the apocryphal Acts of Andrew, John, and others. In between lie the books classified as disputed (James, Jude, 2 Peter, and 2–3 John) and as spurious (Acts of Paul, *Shepherd* of Hermas, Revelation of Peter; Barnabas, Didachai [*sic*.], and perhaps the Revelation of John); some, he says, add the *Gospel of the Hebrews* to this category.

Obviously the main outlines of the canon are clear. There is some question about the Epistle to the Hebrews because Eusebius has heard that the Roman church rejects it (3, 3, 5) and has not checked his information. There is even more question about Revelation, since Eusebius cannot decide where to classify it—or the *Gospel of the Hebrews*.

His basic view is clearly that of the Alexandrians. He regards Mark as a disciple of Peter (referring to the opinion of Clement of Alexandria, 2, 15, 1) and Luke as a disciple of Paul (3, 4, 7). Like Origen, he has his doubts about the *Gospel of the Hebrews*, James, Jude, 2 Peter, and 2–3 John. His category of spurious books partly reflects Origen's later views and partly goes beyond them to reject Barnabas. Origen had doubted the authenticity of the Acts of Paul and the *Shepherd* of Hermas; Clement, but not Origen, had used the Revelation of Peter and the *Didache*. The points at which Eusebius goes beyond Origen are those at which apocalyptic writings (Revelation, Barnabas) are in question. As a representative of the new friendliness between church and state, Eusebius regards eschatology as realized in the Constantinian empire. He quotes Dionysius on the Apocalypse in full but does not check his information about the relatively timeless Epistle to the Hebrews.

We see that the influential list which Eusebius provided was largely based on the views current at Alexandria and Caesarea a generation or two before his time. This is almost to say that in his old age Origen created the final form of the New Testament canon. Of course he did not do so in isolation from the churches in which he taught. But his achievement means that in the shaping of the canon the theological and the literary-historical factors were inseparable. The canon is the product of Alexandrian learning applied to the tradition. We see both kinds of judgment at work in the writings of Origen, Dionysius, and finally Eusebius. When Athanasius of Alexandria, in his festal letter of 367, set forth a New Testament canon identical with the one current today, he was doing no more than summing up the results of his predecessors' researches and conclusions.

XII

The New Testament of the early Church Fathers

We should not suppose that the conclusions of Eusebius or even those of Athanasius, were immediately accepted everywhere by everyone. The *Catechetical Lectures* by Cyril of Jerusalem, delivered in his see city about A.D. 350, show clearly enough that doubts about Revelation, though not about Hebrews, persisted there. Cyril states that there are only four gospels and goes out of his way to attack the *Gospel of Thomas*, which he says was written by the Manichees. 'Perfumed by the sweet smell of the appellation "gospel", it corrupts the souls of simpler believers.' Beyond the gospels are the Acts 'of the twelve apostles'—i.e. only the canonical book, not apocryphal competitors. Then come the seven 'catholic epistles' of James and Peter, John and Jude. The whole New Testament is given a confirmatory seal by the fourteen (thus including Hebrews) epistles of Paul. Cyril adds that all other books are secondary to these, and that books not read in churches are not to be read privately.[1]

An example of rather wild variety is provided by a list, probably from the fourth century, inserted in the Codex Claromontanus (sixth century, containing the Pauline epistles). This list contains all the books of the Bible. Its New Testament consists of four gospels (Matthew, John,

1 *Cat.* 4, 36; PG. 33, 500–1.

Mark, Luke—apostles first, disciples second), the epistles of Paul (Romans, 1–2 Corinthians, Galatians, Ephesians, 1–2 Timothy, Titus, Colossians, Philemon!), 'ad Petrum' 1–2 (!), James, 1–2–3 John, Jude, Barnabas, Revelation of John, Acts, the *Shepherd* (of Hermas), the Acts of Paul, and the Revelation of Peter. The order and number of the Pauline epistles is very peculiar, and the last four works had been— or perhaps were to be—classified as 'spurious' by Eusebius. Zahn thought that about 300 the list came from the environs of Alexandria, where the last four works were certainly read; but it is just as likely that it reflects the usage of some backward community, dependent upon Alexandria, at a later date.

The 'Cheltenham list', probably from about 360 and possibly from North Africa, contains four gospels (Matthew, Mark, John, Luke—as in the 'Curetonian' Syriac version), thirteen epistles of Paul, Acts, Revelation, three epistles of John (or 'only one'), and two epistles of Peter (or 'only one'). The author seems to be combining the usage of his local community with that more typically Syrian, for it was in Syria that only 1 John and 1 Peter were accepted for a long time.

But while variety is characteristic of these lists accidentally preserved, the writings of the great theologians like Athanasius point toward a New Testament essentially uniform. From the late fourth century we possess two versified lists which were accepted at the Council of Constantinople in A.D. 962. One, from Gregory of Nazianzus, states the authenticity of all the New Testament books commonly received, but does not mention Revelation; the other, from Amphilochius of Iconium, is more complex, since it admits that some persons (wrongly) reject Hebrews; some accept only James, 1 Peter, and 1 John, while others add 2–3 John, 2 Peter, and Jude. Amphilochius does not state what his own opinion is. As for Revelation, some accept it, but most people call it spurious. He concludes by claiming that this is 'the most trustworthy canon of the inspired scriptures'— in spite of his refusal to come to a decision about some of the books in dispute. Presumably he did not wish to enter into acrimonious controversy over the four catholic epistles in question.[1]

Even more important than Western doubts about the authenticity of Hebrews were Eastern doubts about the canonicity of the catholic or general epistles ascribed to James, Peter, John, and Jude. Some Eastern writings and writers reflect acceptance of none of them, but since they come from the fourth and fifth centuries we may suspect that this rejection is due to learned theory or considerations of simplicity (perhaps Marcionite or generally Gnostic in origin) rather than to tradition. Most of the Eastern writers accept at least 1 Peter and 1 John, the two accepted by Diodorus of Tarsus and Nestorius and known to Ephrem Syrus. In the Peshitto, the works of John Chrysostom, and those of Theodoret, we find these two and also the letter of James. Semi-mathematical analysis of the possible varieties of usage suggests that the choices are not random. The collection of the general epistles had as its nucleus 1 Peter and 1 John; to these were added (1) the minor Johannine epistle or epistles,[2] (2) either James or Jude, sometimes both of them,[3] and finally (3) 2 Peter.[4] The likelihood that the rejection of all the letters was late is suggested by the fact that the nucleus was known to almost all the Greek Christian writers of the first two centuries after the Apostolic Fathers.

1 For the texts of these passages see F. W. Grosheide, *Some Early Lists of the Books of the New Testament* (Leiden, 1948).

2 Irenaeus; probably Theophilus.

3 Jude: Clement of Alexandria, Tertullian; James: see above.

4 2 Peter is not attested before the time of Origen.

The later development of the canon (the word 'canon' in the sense of 'list' first occurs in the passage from Amphilochius to which we have referred) can be described rather briefly. With the Gnostic crisis long past, the Church was generally free, in the course of the fourth century and the early fifth, to create a canon which would be inclusive rather than exclusive. Among the Latins, James and 2 Peter had at first been unknown or rejected; neither occurs in the Old Latin version or in the Muratorian list. Hebrews, though in the Old Latin version, had not been accepted by Gaius of Rome or Cyprian, and it is not mentioned in the Muratorianum. By the end of the fourth century, Latin writers accepted all these books. At the eastern edge of the Christian world, there continued to be considerable doubt about the book of Revelation and about the general epistles, or at least James, 2 Peter, Jude, and 2–3 John. In both the West and the East, then, previous academic-ecclesiastical decisions played a considerable part. The situation described by Eusebius did not change much.

Finally, however, the West accepted Hebrews and the East accepted the general epistles and the Apocalypse. From the sixth century onwards, except for minor aberrations such as occasional acceptance of the forged letter of Paul to the Laodiceans, Christians regarded the twenty-seven books of the New Testament as canonical.

We have seen that the process of canonization lasted for centuries. Its methodology was not always clear, and the most important factor involved seems to have been prior usage as known to the writers who discussed the subject. Apostolic authorship was often understood rather freely—necessarily so in view of the fact that neither Mark nor Luke was an apostle.

The crucial period in the history of the canon was the second century and the early third, from the time when

Christian writers began to use the New Testament books as authoritative and inspired to the time when they found it necessary to select some books, out of the mass of supposed early Christian literature, and reject others. We do not know what valuable works, now lost, they could have preserved had they wished to do so. We know only what was in fact preserved, and it would appear that this gives us a fairly reliable impression of the Church's life and faith in the first century. If we were to suppose that such a treatise as the *Gospel of Thomas* should have been treated as canonical, we should have to assume that early Christian theology was what it was not, i.e., Gnostic.[1] This is not to say that what was preserved permits us to reconstruct a uniform, monolithic early Christian theology. There was a great deal of variety in the books which most Christians accepted, and the inclusion of further books in East and West during the fourth and fifth centuries meant that the variety was increased. It was necessary, however, for some limits to be set to the flowering of Christian speculation, and such limits were set by insistence upon loyalty to the tradition as classically expressed by the apostles and their disciples. It is this tradition, in written form, which we possess in the New Testament as it stands today.

---

1 Cf. B. Gaertner, *The Theology of the Gospel of Thomas* (New York, 1961).

XIII

The formation of the New Testament

The formation of the New Testament was a process, extending over at least two centuries, in the course of which the oral teaching and preaching of Jesus and the apostles (1) was recorded in written form and was circulated among the Christian churches, (2) was accepted by these churches in certain formulations and not in others, (3) was regarded first as the key to the Old Testament, then as equal to it in authority, and (4) came to be regarded as inspired 'scripture'. The process took place within the Christian communities during the period in which greater clarity and precision were achieved in relation to doctrine, discipline, and worship. The New Testament books came to be regarded as providing norms for doctrine and guidance for Christian behavior; they were read in the course of Christian worship. This situation made it necessary for the churches to determine exactly what was in the New Testament and what was not. There was little doubt about most of the books supposed to have been written by the apostles and their disciples, although members of various sects often rejected individual documents or groups of documents. Gnostics, for example, almost invariably rejected the Pastoral Epistles, since in them something much like Gnosticism was being attacked. The conservative Jewish-Christian Ebionites accepted none of the Pauline epistles. At the other extreme (perhaps), conservative opponents of Montanist prophecy criticized the Gospel of John and Revelation, since the Montanists were appealing to them. But in general second-century Christians regarded as authoritative four gospels, thirteen Pauline epistles, 1 Peter, 1 John, and Revelation (sometimes also the book of Acts).

Real difficulties arose in regard to Hebrews, since it was inadequately attested as written by Paul, and in regard to the minor Catholic epistles, since they had rarely been used by Christians in the early second century. The question of Pauline authorship in the case of Hebrews was overcome, rather than answered, at Alexandria by Christians who knew that the letter had been used in 1 Clement and that, whether precisely Pauline or not, it reflected early Christian theological thinking. It is not clear how James, Jude, and 2 Peter were brought into the authoritative collections. The ideas of James could obviously be related to those of the synoptic gospels; Jude was useful in dealing with heresy; and 2 Peter may have won acceptance because of its author's identification of himself as the author of 1 Peter (2 Pet. 3:1). But we cannot be sure that these reasons were really responsible for the acceptance of the books. On the other hand, the style and the content of 2 and 3 John inevitably led those who accepted the Gospel and 1 John to accept these little letters also.

The most difficult problem of all concerned the various documents which lay beyond the fringe of the Old Testament and the generally accepted collection of New Testament books. The Old Testament itself had not been very clearly defined in the first century, and the Greek version called the Septuagint contains several books which second-century Jews did not accept. In addition, there were many apocalypses in circulation, some of them used by New Testament writers, and these books too were rejected by most Jews in the second century. Christian writers, though with some hesitation, continued to employ them. Again, since the formation of the New Testament was a gradual process, oral traditions supposedly derived from Jesus and the apostles, as well as books containing such traditions, were used by most second-century Christians along with the books generally accepted. Very few writers refrained from using both oral traditions and one or more of the apocryphal gospels, acts, epistles, and apocalypses.

The grounds on which acceptance or rejection took place were not very clearly defined. In essence, there were two such grounds. (1) A book had either been handed down traditionally or it had not. This test, when based on anything beyond assertion by the leader of a Christian community, involved research in the church libraries which we see emerging at the end of the second century and the beginning of the third (though obviously smaller collections existed at an earlier time). The conclusions of administrators and scholars, doubtless related to the memories of the older members of the communities, were presumably correct, generally speaking, but in relation to individual documents whose authority was being questioned there was obviously room for error. Second-century Christian leaders traveled a good deal. The extent of their travels implies not only that local differences would tend to be minimized but also that local differences would tend to be forgotten. This is to say that 'tradition' in regard to particular books almost means 'actual situation' in regard to them. (2) A book was either written by an apostle, or by a disciple of an apostle, or it was not. This is to say that the title of a book, inscribed at its beginning or end, was very important. The title had a presumption in its favor. To be sure, modern scholars sometimes tend to suppose that this notion is wrong, and that the titles of New Testament books have practically no claim to acceptance. Obviously such external testimony can be wrong; but one might do worse than to agree with Bishop Light-foot (1876): 'If there is substantial ground for suspicion, the suspicion has its weight, but not otherwise.'[1] We should hold that the early Christians were right when they tended to accept writings ascribed to apostles as apostolic. It must be admitted, however, that various kinds of tests needed to be applied to the documents in question, and that the arguments of Christians like Irenaeus, Julius Africanus, Origen, and Dionysius of Alexandria show that the tests were some-times being applied. These tests, based on textual, literary, and historical analysis, do not always lead to conclusive results but (with or without the use of computers) they are all we have. Unfortunately, it does not appear that early Christians often or, indeed, usually applied them. Their ideas about what was or was not apostolic seem to have been based on the general idea that, since they themselves were maintaining the apostolic faith, whatever was not in harmony with their understanding of it cannot have been apostolic. Ideas of doctrinal variety or development were not generally accepted, in spite of Origen's insistence upon the notion that in some respects doctrine did develop.

If we admit the seriousness of the difficulties latent in early Christian notions about the continuity of tradition and the question of apostolic authorship, it is fairly clear that, whatever Christians in the late second century may have supposed, the selection and 'canonization' of New Testament documents was partly the product of late second-century attitudes. Certainly these attitudes were not *simply* second-century attitudes; they were based on the life and thought of previous generations of Christians. At the same

1 Quoted by J. M. Cotterill, *Modern Criticism and Clement's Epistles to Virgins* (Edinburgh, 1884), 59.

time, however, they were based on the widespread, almost universal, presupposition that Christianity had remained precisely what it had been from the beginning; and this presupposition was maintained by denying that heretics, especially Gnostic heretics, had based their faith or their knowledge upon older traditions. This denial is open to question, since it would appear that both Gnostics and more orthodox Christians often diverged from a common starting-point, and that some heresies (e.g. Judaistic Christianity) in part reflected a form of Christian thinking later outmoded.

In order to avoid these difficulties, we should regard the New Testament as the product of the 'great Church' which transcended local differences. The books of the New Testament, not necessarily always accepted by everyone, were those which came to be universally accepted by the overwhelming majority of Christians; the same books, not necessarily apostolic, were those which commended themselves as reflecting the basic beliefs of the earliest Church.

It may appear that by treating the history of canonization in this way we are undercutting the authority of both the New Testament and the Church. Such is not the case, however, for we should regard both the New Testament and the Church as having been brought into existence in response to the life and work of Jesus, who in the view of Christians was God's incarnate Word. When we use the word 'response' it may seem that we are treating the New Testament and the Church as human products and nothing more. Admittedly, and certainly, we are treating them as human products, for that is what they indisputably are. But from the standpoint of Christian theology there are no products of this kind that are not human. The 'divine initiative' can doubtless exist apart from human responses (the creation of the universe provides an obvious example), but the life of the Church and the witness of the New Testament books cannot (theologically speaking) be viewed as in any sense divine apart from their 'humanity'. The 'divine human encounter' has to be a real encounter, with two parties involved.

It may also appear that the authority of New Testament and Church comes to be rather circular. The Church uses the documents it has selected in order to provide its own credentials. The documents are chosen so as to prove what the Church wants proved. Here we can only agree. The authority *is* circular. The point, however, is that both Church and New Testament are only secondary authorities. They are circular in that they lie on the edge of a circle drawn around the center, which is Christ. The authority of Christ, mediated through his apostles, was expressed in both Church and New Testament. The Church interprets the New Testament; in turn, the New Testament reminds the Church of the nature of the apostolic testimony and can correct the Church's presentation of the gospel.

The early history of the formation of the New Testament does not suggest that all parts of it possessed equal authority, any more than the history of the Church suggests that all Christians have possessed equal authority. There was a central core of New Testament books, consisting of the four gospels and thirteen Pauline epistles, and it is very clear that these books were accepted both earlier and more generally than the other books were. We may like to think that James, for example, provides as good a witness to the essence of Christianity as the major Pauline epistles do. Second-century Christians, it is clear, did not think so. On the other hand, the fact that books like James and Jude and 2 Peter finally came to be recognized as belonging to the New Testament indicates that there were aspects of these books which most Christians considered important, if only for the sake of balance and—even—variety. A canon from which these books were absent would suggest that Christianity is narrower and more uniform than is actually the case. Those who claim that 2 Peter, for example, brings 'Greek' elements into Christian thinking are neglecting the extent to which it actually is, and should be, Greek as well as 'Hebrew'.

Finally, historically valuable though the apocryphal books are in providing information about the ideas of sectarian groups and their ideas of tradition—and perhaps in some instances for preserving first-century materials—those who believe that in general the Church was right as against its opponents cannot reverse its decisions about these documents. The apocryphal books reflect responses to Jesus, but the kinds of responses they contain are usually severely conditioned both by their authors' notions that they understand Jesus better than the apostles did and by the view that he really wanted to convey an esoteric spiritual doctrine which the Church's gospels do not set forth. Usually these authors deny his humanity, thus cutting him (and themselves) off both from the historical life of the Church and from the historical life of mankind.

It is in the New Testament, and the New Testament alone, that we find the written record of the apostolic response to the life of Jesus, though it is in the Church (with all its imperfections) that this response continues, or can continue, to be expressed.

Select Bibliography

Aland, K. *The Problem of the New Testament Canon*. London, 1962

Allegro, J. M. 'Fragments of a Qumran Scroll of Eschatological Midrāšim', *Journal of Biblical Literature* 77 (1958), 350–4

Allegro, J. M. 'Further Messianic References in Qumran Literature', *Journal of Biblical Literature* 75 (1956), 174–87

Audet, J.-P. *La Didachè: instructions des apôtres*. Paris, 1958

Audet, J.-P. 'A Hebrew-Aramaic List of Books of the Old Testament in Greek Transcription', *Journal of Theological Studies* 1 (1950), 135–54

Barth, C. 'Die Interpretationen des Neuen Testaments in der Valentinianischen Gnosis', *Texte und Untersuchungen* 37, 3. Leipzig, 1911

Barthélemy, D. 'Redécouverte d'un chaînon manquant de l'histoire de la Septante', *Revue Biblique* 60 (1953), 18–29

Bell, H. I.–Skeat, T. C. *Fragments of an Unknown Gospel and other Early Christian Papyri*. London, 1935

Benoit, A. 'Irénée Adversus haereses IV 17, et les Testimonia', *Texte und Untersuchungen* 79 (1961), 20–7

Blackman, E. C. *Marcion and his Influence*. London, 1948

Campenhausen, H. von. 'Polycarp von Smyrna und die Pastoralbriefe', *Sitzungsberichte der Heidelberger Akademie der Wissenschaften* (Philos.-hist. Kl.), 1951, no. 2

Cross, F. L. (ed.). *The Jung Codex*. London, 1955

Dahl, N. A. 'Welche Ordnung der Paulusbriefe wird vom Muratorischen Kanon vorausgesetzt?', *Zeitschrift für die neutestamentliche Wissenschaft* 52 (1961), 39–53

Daniélou, J. 'Les traditions secrètes des Apôtres', *Eranos-Jahrbuch* 31 (1962), 199–215

Goodspeed, E. J. *The Formation of the New Testament*. Chicago, 1926

Goodspeed, E. J. *The Meaning of Ephesians*. Chicago, 1933

Grant, R. M. *The Apostolic Fathers* I. New York, 1964

Grant, R. M. *The Apostolic Fathers* II (with H. H. Graham). New York, 1965

Grant, R. M. *The Earliest Lives of Jesus*. London–New York, 1961

Grant, R. M. *Gnosticism: an Anthology*. London–New York, 1961

Grant, R. M. *The Letter and the Spirit*. London, 1957

Grant, R. M. *The Secret Sayings of Jesus* (with D. N. Freedman and W. R. Schoedel). New York–London, 1960

Grant, R. M. *A Short History of the Interpretation of the Bible* (revised edition). New York, 1964; London, 1965

Grant, R. M. 'The Fragments of the Greek Apologists and Irenaeus', J. N. Birdsall–R. W. Thomson (eds.), *Biblical and Patristic Studies in Memory of Robert Pierce Casey* (Freiburg, 1963), 179–218

Grant, R. M. 'Hermeneutics and Tradition in Ignatius of Antioch', E. Castelli (ed.), *Ermeneutica e tradizione* (Rome, 1963), 183–201

Grant, R. M. 'Like Children', *Harvard Theological Review* 39 (1946), 71–3

Grant, R. M. 'Tatian (*Or.* 30) and the Gnostics', *Journal of Theological Studies* 15 (1964), 65–9

Grosheide, F. W. *Some Early Lists of the Books of the New Testament*. Leiden, 1948

Gutwenger, E. 'The Anti-Marcionite Prologues', *Theological Studies* 7 (1946), 393–409

Hanson, R. P. C. *Origen's Doctrine of Tradition*. London, 1954

Harnack, A. *Das Neue Testament um das Jahre 200*. Freiburg, 1889

Harnack, A. 'Marcion: das Evangelium vom fremden Gott' (2nd ed.), *Texte und Untersuchungen* 45. Leipzig, 1924

Heard, R. G. 'The Old Gospel Prologues', *Journal of Theological Studies* 6 (1955), 1–16

Jacquier, E. *Le Nouveau Testament dans l'Eglise chrétienne* I (2nd ed.). Paris, 1911

Jülicher, A.–Fascher, E. *Einleitung in das Neue Testament* (7th ed.), Tübingen, 1931, 451–558

Katz, P. 'The Old Testament Canon in Palestine and Alexandria', *Zeitschrift für die neutestamentliche Wissenschaft* 47 (1956), 191–217

Knox, J. *Marcion and the New Testament*. Chicago, 1942

Knox, J. *Philemon among the Letters of Paul*. Chicago, 1935

Koester, H. 'Synoptische Ueberlieferungen bei den Apostolischen Vätern', *Texte und Untersuchungen* 65. Berlin, 1957

Koester, H. 'Die aüsserkanonischen Herrenworte', *Zeitschrift für die neutestamentliche Wissenschaft* 48 (1957), 220–37

Leipoldt, J. *Geschichte des neutestamentlichen Kanons* (2 vol.). Leipzig, 1907–8

Lietzmann, H. 'Wie wurden die Bücher des Neuen Testaments heilige Schrift?' *Texte und Untersuchungen* 68 (Berlin, 1958), 15–98

Maurer, C. *Ignatius von Antiochien und das Johannesevangelium.* Zürich, 1949

Mayeda, G. *Das Leben-Jesu-Fragment Papyrus Egerton* 2. Berne, 1946

Perler, O. 'Das vierte Makkabaeerbuch, Ignatius von Antiochien und die aeltesten Martyrerberichte', *Rivista di archeologia cristiana* 25 (1949), 47–72

Quispel, G. *Ptolémée: Lettre à Flora.* Paris, 1949

Roberts, C. H. *An Unpublished Fragment of the Fourth Gospel.* Manchester, 1935

Ruwet, J. 'Clément d'Alexandrie, Canon des Écritures et Apocryphes', *Biblica* 29 (1948), 240–71

Ruwet, J. 'Les apocryphes dans l'œuvre d'Origène', *Biblica* 23 (1942), 18–42; 24 (1943), 18–58; 25 (1944), 143–66

Ryle, H. E. *The Canon of the Old Testament.* London, 1892

Sagnard, F. M. *Clément d'Alexandrie: Extraits de Théodote.* Paris 1948

Smith, M. See *New York Times*, 30 December 1960

Sundberg, A. C., Jr. 'The Old Testament of the Early Church', *Harvard Theological Review* 51 (1958), 205–26

Testuz, M. *Papyrus Bodmer* V. Geneva, 1958

Testuz, M. *Papyrus Bodmer* VII–IX. Geneva, 1959

Testuz, M. *Papyrus Bodmer* X–XII. Geneva, 1959

Testuz, M. *Papyrus Bodmer* XIII. Geneva, 1960

Van Unnik, W. C. 'The "Gospel of Truth" and the New Testament'. F. L. Cross (ed.), *The Jung Codex* (London, 1955), 79–129

Van Unnik, W. C. ''Η καινὴ διαθήκη—a Problem in the early history of the Canon', *Texte und Untersuchungen* 79 (Berlin, 1961), 212–27

Werner, J. 'Der Paulinismus des Irenaeus', *Texte und Untersuchungen* 6, 2. Leipzig, 1889

Zahn, T. *Forschungen zur Geschichte des neutestamentlichen Kanons und der altkirchlichen Literatur* (10 vols.). Erlangen, 1881–1929

Zahn, T. *Grundriss der Geschichte des neutestamentlichen Kanons* (2nd ed.). Leipzig, 1904

Index

B—MODERN SCHOLARS